COME FLY WITH US!

A Global History of the Airline Hostess

Johanna Omelia & Michael Waldock

COME FLY WITH US!

A Global History of the Airline Hostess

Johanna Omelia & Michael Waldock

PORTLAND, OREGON

This book is dedicated to
flight attendants everywhere.

The authors will donate a portion of their profits to

The Flight Attendant Disaster Relief Fund, which was

established by the Association of Flight Attendants.

Library of Congress Cataloging-in-Publication Data

Waldock, Michael 1939 -
Omelia, Johanna 1959 -
Come fly with us! : a global history of the airline hostess / By Johanna
Omelia and Michael Waldock.
    p. cm.
      ISBN 1-888054-61-1 (hardcover)
1. Flight attendants-History. I. Title.
HD8039.A43 O45 2003
387.7'42--dc21

          2002015142

Book Design Wade Daughtry, Collectors Press, Inc.
Editor Peggy Lindquist

For a free catalog write to:

COLLECTORS PRESS, INC.

P.O. Box 230986
Portland, OR 97281
Toll Free 1 800 423 1848
collectorspress.com

Printed in Singapore

9 8 7 6 5 4 3 2 1

Contents

Adrian Meridith/British Airways Archives.

Foreword and Acknowledgments

Courtesy Airbus.

From flying nurse to geisha to the professionals of today, flight attendants have come a long way. We celebrate them and their accomplishments. With a vast and international project, there are many people and companies we'd like to thank in the creation of this book. We could not have done it without eBay where many of the images, uniforms, and collateral materials were found. We'd like to thank models Alexandra Hagedorn, Isabel Tapia, and makeup artist Lora Condon, makeupwithme.com; proofreaders Lisa Perry, Solena Rawdah, Jan Goodwin, Mary Jane Tenerelli; information gatherers and providers Justin Collin, Michael Conti, Durward Cruickshank, Karli Hagedorn, Barbara Lewnowski, Bob Maich, Michael O'Melia, Rosie Oppenheim, Maggie Phinney, Anne Roberts, Leslie Sena, Lisa Thomen, Alison Thompson, Kathleen Wakefield, Nick Waldock, and Kay Wild. Former American Airlines' flight attendant Lois Maguire Wisniewski and PSA's Deborah Lewandowski, Cyndee Irvine, and Deborah Norris; local Santa Fe businesses, Santa Fe Executive Aviation, and Vicky at Camera and Darkroom; and Dawn Deeks at the Association of Flight Attendants. Adobe Photoshop geniuses Tom Gaukel and Laura Shaia, and translator Lena Ackermann. We'd also like to thank the following executives in public relations, communications, marketing, and archives:

Aeroflot – Tatiana Leonova
Airbus Industrie – Maryanne Greczyn & Mark Luginbill
Air Canada – Caterina Trotto
Air France – Aurélien Gomez
Alaska Airlines – Danna Maros
American Airlines C.R. Smith Museum – Ben Kristy
American Airlines, Inc. – Mayda Wells
American Express Company – Diane Cahill
Ansett Australia – Annie Tahami
Braniff (Dallas Historical Society) – Rachel Roberts

Braniff International – Harding Lawrence
British Airways/Adrian Meredith – Paula Doran and Kirsty Tillyer
Cathay Pacific – Carina Chow and Rosita Ng
China Airlines – Vera Su
The Coca-Cola Company – Bruce Proctor and Richard Robinson
Continental Airlines – Mark Eichberger
Cosmopolitan magazine, the Hearst Corporation – Abigail Greene
Delta Air Transport Heritage Museum – Marie Keck and Paulette O'Donnell
Esquire magazine – Makina Davis
Finnair – Tuija Silvas
Japan Airlines – Irene Jackson Schon
JetBlue Airways – Gareth Edmonson-Jones
Life/Time Inc. – Rona Tuccillo
LTU International Airways – Marco Dadomo
Lufthansa – Oliver Bartelmeh
Malaysia Airlines – Shauqi Ahmad
Northwest Airlines – Cindy Choate
Parade – Lee Kravitz and Marva Shearer
Qantas – Josephine Fasullo and Des Sullivan
SAS – Anne Bergstrand
Southwest – Linda Jones
Stan Herman Studio – Stan Herman and Michael Schwarz
Swissair – Marlyse Bartis
TAP-Air Portugal – Adelina Arezes
THAI – Sunathee Isvarphornchai
TWA LLC/American Airlines, Inc. – Karl McAfee and Mayda Wells
United Airlines – Barbara Hanson and Joe Hopkins
US Airways – Richard Weintraub

Fasten Your Seatbelts; the Adventure of Air Travel

Flying in the early years was quite an adventure. Planes were not pressurized, cabins were not soundproofed, and passengers had to put up with weather extremes and altitude chill. There was no radar system in place and no way to ascertain weather conditions in various cities. If a pilot saw thunder clouds rolling in, he'd land in a field and wait out the storm among the cow pastures or in the desert. Flying was only conducted during the day, as the runways and routes in the U.S. weren't lighted from coast to coast until the end of the 1920s. At the dawn of commercial aviation, the top cruising speed of propeller planes was 125 mph and low-flying altitudes, well under 10,000 feet, ensured that flight conditions were wildly turbulent. Passenger comfort was hardly a consideration, as airplanes around the world were used primarily for the lucrative business of transporting mail in the 1920s, mostly in converted World War I planes.

The First Air Mail Routes

In the USA, Congress gave the Postmaster General the power to plan the first networks of air mail routes. In 1918, the first air mail run was conducted between Washington, D.C., and New York. Two years later, President Wilson officiated over the ceremony in which the country's first coast to coast air mail service, called U.S. Air Mail Route No. 1, was celebrated. Starting in 1926, the various routes were assigned to private contractors, establishing the country's first airlines, Boeing Air Transport (BAT), later known as United Air Lines, Eastern Air Lines, American Airlines, and Transcontinental and Western Airlines (TWA).

Airlines accommodated the occasional passenger but, in the early days, trains were generally a faster, far cheaper and more reliable mode of travel. A flight from coast to coast took 32 hours and required 14 refueling stops en route, barring mechanical or weather delays. Food was rarely available at stop-over points, and forced landings were such a standard event that pilots carried railroad timetables as backup for their passengers.

Early European and Australian Passenger Planes

Conditions for European passenger travel were similarly austere. British Airways forerunner Aircraft Transport and Travel Limited (AT&T) launched the world's first daily international scheduled air service between London and Paris in 1919. The de Havilland Airco 4A biplane carried a single passenger and cargo that often included newspapers, Devonshire Cream, and grouse. Usually, the flight took two hours, but one pilot took two days to complete the route, making 33 forced landings along the way.

In Australia, Qantas made its first scheduled flight in 1922, a 580-mile trip carrying one passenger. The pilot, Wilmot Hudson Fysh, stated that the sight of men in goggles and flight suits landing their airplane at the local race course caused a lot of excitement from the local population. "It created the [same] sensation an astronaut in a space suit would make if he suddenly appeared in a country town," he reportedly reminisced. The trip that took about eight hours of flying over two days in 1922 is routinely covered by Qantas in one hour today.

Early air passengers flew in tiny biplanes and were given flying helmets, goggles, and parachutes to wear. They stuffed their ears with cotton to protect them from the engine noise and chewed gum to help clear their ears, which were blocked from the effects of altitude. They were weighed before boarding, as the pilot had to calculate the aircraft's weight and balance before take-off. Cabins were small and passengers often sat on mailbags.

No refreshments were served unless a kindly pilot shared coffee from his own thermos. Passengers often succumbed to airsickness. But whatever ailments they suffered, they were on their own.

In-Flight Service Launched with Cabin Boys

In 1922, Britain's Daimler Airways, a successor to AT&T, hired the world's first stewards, who were called "cabin boys." Soon, stewards were fixtures on flights throughout the world.

The jobs of these boys, characterized by Daimler as "alert, good-looking youngsters," in the first few years were to weigh and load passengers and mail, check passengers in, and, in the late 1920s, to pass out boxed lunches of fried chicken. The lads also offered a good dose of moral support, a priceless commodity for the early air travelers.

In 1930, in-flight service was revolutionized. And it started with Ellen Church, a diminutive young woman with big ideas.

Credit: "Air California"

Ch 1

The
1930s

Nurses Become the First Stewardesses

The **first stewardesses** fixed loose chairs, loaded baggage, discussed meteorology and sights with nervous passengers, and occasionally touched up the plane between flights! Credit: "United Airlines Archives"

On May 15, 1930, Cresco, Iowa-born Ellen Church made aviation history as the world's first stewardess, flying for Boeing Air Transport (later United Air Lines) from Oakland, California, to Chicago, Illinois. The previous year, Church had approached Steve Stimpson, BAT's District Traffic Manager in San Francisco, for a job on an airplane. A registered nurse, Church pointed out that she was well qualified to assist ailing passengers on the bumpy flights. Stimpson wrote a note to his boss, which read in part, "Imagine the psychology of having young women as part of the crew. Imagine the national publicity we could get from it and the tremendous effect it would have on the traveling public. Also imagine the value they would be to us, not only in the neater and nicer method of serving food, but looking out for the passengers' welfare." Stimpson was turned down flat initially, but he persevered. Soon permission was granted to sign on Church as Chief Stewardess and seven additional nurses to represent United.

The "Original Eight" were trained as stewardesses, a name United copyrighted in 1934. To underscore their professionalism, the stewardesses donned a uniform, a dark green double-breasted wool suit with silver buttons. A wool cape was also worn to keep the women warm in drafty cabins. The cape featured pockets large enough to hold a railroad timetable, a wrench, and a screwdriver to secure the passengers' wicker chairs to the floor. The ensemble was topped with a wool "shower-cap" tam.

Farm Girls and Baronesses: Famous Women Pilots

By the 1930s, women in the air were no longer a novelty. The Baroness de la Roche of France was the first licensed woman pilot in the world. Harriet Quimby of Coldwater, Massachusetts, became the first American woman to qualify for a license from the Aero Club of America in 1911 and was celebrated for becoming the first woman pilot to fly across the English Channel in early 1912.

Kansas-born Amelia Earhart was America's sweetheart in the 1930s. She crossed the Atlantic alone in 1932, and her flight from Newfoundland to Ireland in 14 hours, 56 minutes set a new record. Earhart was also the first person to make a successful solo flight from Hawaii to California in 1935. She disappeared over the central Pacific in a twin engine Lockheed Electra in 1937, two-thirds of the way through flying around the world.

England's Amy Johnson was another pioneering aviator who set records throughout the decade. In 1930, Johnson became famous for her flight from England to Australia in a tiny Gipsy Moth biplane she named Jason. The following year, she became the first pilot to fly from London to Moscow in one day, continuing on to Tokyo. So loved was Johnson that she inspired a popular song, "Amy, Wonderful Amy," which started:

> *"Amy, wonderful Amy*
> *How can you blame me*
> *For loving you…"*

Florida-born Jacqueline Cochran, too, was flying in the 1930s, and proved herself to be one of the world's greatest pilots, setting numerous records. Cochran was also responsible for organizing and directing the Women's Airforce Service Pilots (WASPs) during World War II. New Zealander Jean Batten gained her commercial pilot's license in 1932 and set records for her flights from England to Australia, and numerous other women were also regarded as aviation pioneers and national heroes.

A

B

C

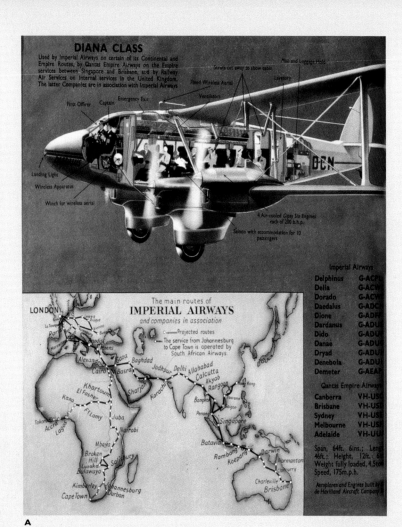

Illustrated is a Fokker F-10-A Super-Tri-Motor, which carries 12 passengers and 2 pilots.

GENERAL MOTORS CHOSE FOKKER

SHOULDN'T YOU?

PROBABLY no study ever made of the aircraft industry excelled in thoroughness the one conducted by General Motors Corporation. This world-famed institution, desirous of extending its interests to include airplane manufacture, pursued its search for an ideal affiliation with all the vast scientific and technical resources at its command. Its examination revealed one name glowing imperishably in the skies. That name was Fokker.

You may not know that Fokker has designed and built more airplanes than any other manufacturer in the world. You may not know that Fokker planes have made twice as many

pioneering long-distance and trans-oceanic flights as have any other make. You may not know that Fokkers have flown more than *twenty-five million miles* on regular transport schedules, matchlessly dependable. But General Motors, fixedly intent on lending its strength where it was best deserved, knew these and other things. General Motors chose Fokker . . . Shouldn't you? Then ask for a Fokker when you fly.

Fokker manufacture now includes ten different models of airplanes: single and multi-engined types, land planes, sea planes, flying boats, amphibions. Because of economies due to production principles of General Motors, prices are probably lower than you might expect. Convenient terms may now be arranged on the GMAC finance plan. Requests for information or demonstration are invited, and will be promptly answered. Address Fokker Aircraft Corporation of America, General Motors Building, New York.

FOKKER

AFFILIATED WITH GENERAL MOTORS CORPORATION

D

FLY AMERICAN'S
Southern Sunshine Route
to the
Sun Country
OVERNIGHT

FOR RESERVATIONS OR INFORMATION, CALL YOUR TRAVEL AGENT OR AMERICAN AIRLINES, INC.

AMERICAN AIRLINES *Inc.*

224 E. Wisconsin   MILWAUKEE   Marquette 3830

A M E R I C A N   A I R L I N E S ,   I N C .

E

A

A

In 1936, this major women's magazine featured
a stewardess on its front cover, and a dramatic
hostess-as-heroine story inside. Credit: Cosmopolitan
magazine, the Hearst Corporation.

Initially, U.S. pilots and some passengers were skeptical about the worth of the original stewardesses, but soon the industry accepted them as an integral part of the aviation family. Some regular passengers even called ahead to confirm that their favorite stewardess would be working on their flight. United's bookings increased substantially after the "Original Eight" were introduced.

Slim, Young, and Friendly; Requirements for Sky Girls

Requirements and qualifications for stewardesses were established. The women had to be single, under 25 years old, a maximum of 5'4", reflecting the low ceilings and narrow aisles of the early aircrafts' interiors. 20/20 vision was mandatory, and the stewardesses had to weigh less than 115 pounds as extra weight meant that less revenue-earning mail could be carried, and a slender figure could negotiate the narrow aisles. Pilots were to weigh stewardesses to ensure compliance.

Weight was such an issue in the early 1930s that passengers were often asked to sit forward in the cabin to prevent heaviness in the tail. One stewardess recalled that the pilot could always tell when a passenger got up to move around because the entire plane "did a dance!"

At United, the Do's and Don'ts for the original "sky girls" included a requirement for the stewardess to treat the pilot and copilot with strict formality: "a rigid military salute will be rendered the captain and copilot as they go aboard and deplane the passengers."

B

C

A

And a useful hint on deportment: "Face the rear of the cabin when talking with passengers or serving lunch. Bending over while facing the front of the plane tends to place the seat of your pants in the passenger's face. Tuck your skirt in carefully and assume a ladylike squatting position beside the passenger when carrying on a conversation."

Tread Softly and Carry a Fly Swatter

The "Original Eight" had other responsibilities in the cabin that were outlined in the 1930 Stewardess Manual. "Check the floor bolts on the wicker seats in the Ford Trimotor to make sure they are securely fastened down. Swat flies in cabin after take off. Warn passengers against throwing lighted smoking butts or other objects out the windows, particularly over populated areas."

On long night flights, the stewardesses were to offer passengers slippers. "Assist the passenger to remove his shoes if he so desires. Clean the shoes thoroughly before returning them to him. So as not to startle a passenger when awakening him, touch him gently on the shoulder and if that does not work, tweak his elbow sharply...that is guaranteed to wake him."

One of the most important tasks was to make sure passengers who wanted to use the lavatory didn't use the exit door by mistake! Stewardesses in the 1930s still carried a railroad timetable in case the plane was grounded and passengers needed to resume their journeys by rail. Part of the stewardess' job was to accompany stranded passengers to railroad stations.

More Hostesses Hired

In 1933, Eastern hired seven air hostesses to work on its 18-passenger Curtis Condors. The young women who signed up were hired on a year's probationary period. Soon after, American Airlines hired four nurses to serve as its first "attendants." Swissair was the first European carrier to hire an air hostess in 1934. Her name was Nelly Diener and she died the same year when the Lockheed Orion she was working in crashed. This kind of tragedy was common in the early years of flying, and many stewardesses were killed in crashes or died trying to save their passengers. The nurse/stewardess was the unsung heroine of aviation.

B

In 1936, **sleeper planes** made air travel more comfortable. Here, a United stewardess brings a passenger breakfast in bed. Credit: "United Airlines Archives"

More Comfortable Planes Mean More Passengers

As conditions in the air improved, ticket sales rose 30 percent. Planes were being constructed of metal, a far sturdier material than the wood and fabric fliers of the previous decade. By 1936, TWA had introduced the forerunner to the DC 3 twin engine plane which carried 21 passengers and featured innovations like auto pilot and wing flaps. Some were outfitted as super luxury liners with upholstered wing chairs; others became sleeper planes. Years earlier in Europe, Luft Hansa operated a 12-engine Dornier Do X flying boat, a triple-decker which carried 70 passengers and had dining rooms, bars, and sleeper cabins.

Fresh Air, Writing Paper, and Chewing Gum

A TWA in-flight pamphlet called "At Your Service" outlined the new luxuries available aboard and the many services provided by the air hostess:

Heating
Cabin steam-heated. Hostess will regulate temperature to passengers' comfort.

Ventilators
Cool, fresh air is available from the individual ventilators over the windows.

Want to Read…or Write?
Hostess will gladly give you a choice of popular magazines from the ship's library…Writing paper, writing tables, telegraph blanks…available from hostess. Letters written in flight will be air-mailed by hostess without charge.

Chewing Gum
Obtainable from hostess. Recommended as one means of equalizing air pressure on eardrums.

Lines to a lady about to take the air!

The truth is, this High Life you hear about is nothing but travel reduced to its simplest terms. You practically just put on your hat and go. A trip by plane takes less everything . . . less time, less getting ready, less discomfort on the way.

What shall I wear?

As to clothes, whatever-you happen-to-have. Tweeds and knits and rough silks that don't crumple are nicest. A hat that hugs the hair is comforting, and a warm coat in winter time when you step out of the warmed cabin. Have powder and lipstick and a clean handkerchief in your hand-bag; there's no chance to fiddle with your major luggage after it's packed away. Figure to hold your baggage to thirty-five pounds. That's a good sized bag.

May I talk and smoke

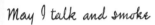

Conversation may be carried on with ordinary Bostonian modulations and you will find interesting, congenial fellow travelers aloft. Time was when you had to scream above the roar of the motors, but voyagers in the new Mainliners chat enjoyably. You may smoke, except immediately before landing and taking off. Electric signs will advise you about that.

Do I really sleep?

Unless your past sins keep you awake, there's no reason why you shouldn't slumber. Tuck yourself into the deep reclining chairs and doze off in the sweet freshness of the clean, silent, upper air. The new planes ride as smoothly as a train, and air conditioning experts have worked out a system that changes the air in the cabin every 45 seconds. It is never stuffy nor drafty, and the temperature is comfortable, no matter what the season.

Where do I eat?

Food appears from a spacious galley, and the attractive stewardess whisks it before you on your individual table. You'll probably be hungry and enjoy it thoroughly . . . dilly-dallying across the sky in a 3-mile-a-minute plane is apt to whet your appetite to an appreciative edge.

Shall I take the children?

. . . Well, why not take them? THEY love it, and are usually as good as gold. How old do youngsters have to be to fly? Well, one young mother took her 12-day old son with her and said the trip was "just a good nap for baby." You can stow the little darlings into a plane, and as soon as you've started you're practically there . . . which simplifies things both for the children and for you! United's stewardess-nurses provide the food the youngsters need and amuse them enroute.

How does it feel to fly?

There is no sensation of great speed in a United plane even though your trip is unbelievably fast. The country seemingly unrolls smoothly, slowly under you. Your pilots in their own compartment are kept constantly in touch with such mundane affairs as the weather by radio telephone. A directive radio beam marks the airway course, beacon lights point like giant fingers, you drift off to sleep feeling that you're touching shoulders with the stars!

Which route?

Cross-continent, United Air Lines flies the popular, advantageous Mid-continent route. New York, Philadelphia, Cleveland and Chicago to the Pacific Coast. At Salt Lake lines radiate like spokes from a wheel to deliver you at the Pacific Coast city you choose . . . another advantage of flying on a line that cuts across the heart of America. You can travel northwesterly from Salt Lake to Seattle, Portland Tacoma and Spokane, due West to San Francisco and to Los Angeles, or direct from Salt Lake to Los Angeles.

About information and reservations

It is just as easy to get a plane ticket these days as ordering a taxicab or a train ticket. You can either make reservations by telephoning United Air Lines and picking up your tickets at the airport, or have them delivered to you. Call the local United office or ask the transportation porter at a hotel or travel bureau to take care of reservations if you wish, or either Postal or Western Union can give you the schedules and deliver tickets to you. No charge for their services. Cabs or limousines take you out to the airports and deliver you downtown when you arrive.

A

B

A
United targeted fashionable women with its brochure, "So You've Never Flown Before," reassuring them that air travel was safe, speedy.

B
Public relations campaigns to assure passengers that air travel was safe and enjoyable ran through the decade. A game of cards and a smoke was always a

C
Much admired first lady Eleanor Roosevelt extolled the virtues of air travel for all Americans. Credit: "United States Airlines and Manufacturers"

Within the photograph:

"WOMEN, AS WELL AS MEN, SHOULD LOOK UPON TRAVELING BY AIR AS UPON ANY OTHER MODE OF TRANSPORTATION"

Eleanor Roosevelt

.... from Eleanor Roosevelt's popular column "My Day"—courtesy United Feature Syndicate

First Lady of the Land, First Lady of the Air, who has enjoyed the refreshing ease and comfort, the time - and money-saving economy of almost 100,000 miles of air travel in the past four years. Mrs. Roosevelt says: "I never cease to marvel at the airplane."

c

Snacks!
Between meals, your hostess will gladly prepare a cup of
coffee, hot chocolate, bouillon, tea…and serve it with tea
wafers or saltines and cheese.

Need a Pick-up?
Your TWA hostess (registered nurse) has a supply of aspirin,
soda tablets, Alka-Seltzer, Hexylresorcinol, Sodium-Amytal,
Ammonia Capsules, Rubbing Alcohol, and Sea Caps (air
sickness prevention) and will be happy to serve you.

Trains Versus Planes

The public still had to be wooed by the airlines to get
over its collective fear of flying. Trains were the main
competition for the airline industry and were generally
a safer, cheaper, and more comfortable method of
transportation. In 1935, planes carried 52,000
passengers. The same year, trains carried 700 million
passengers!

What Shall I Wear? Airlines Target Women Travelers

In a 1937 promotional pamphlet entitled "So you've
never traveled by air before?" United targeted women
travelers, promoting their Douglas Mainliners and
sleeper planes for long-distance flights and their 21-pas-
senger Douglases and 10-passenger Boeings for intercity
flights. Issues like "Where do I eat?" and "May I talk
and smoke?" are tackled in the handout, as are other
topics deemed to be near and dear to a woman's heart:

A

A
Northwest Airlines **hired its first stewardess in 1939.**
Credit: "Courtesy of Northwest Airlines"

B
The glamour and convenience of air travel is captured in
American Airlines' rendering of a **Sky Sleeper** at dawn. Credit:

"SKYSLEEPER AT DAWN"
(American Airlines, Flagship Skysleeper—1936)
Douglas DST.....Two 1100 H. P.
Wright "Cyclone" Engines

This advertisement is one of a series dedicated to the transport companies which have made American commercial aviation the finest in the world. Thompson Products, Inc., manufacturers of Automobile and Aircraft Parts. Cleveland—Detroit.

B

What Shall I Wear?

As to clothes, whatever you happen to have. Tweeds and knits and rough silks are nicest. A hat that hugs the hair is comforting and a warm coat in wintertime when you step out of the warmed cabin. Have powder and lipstick and a clean handkerchief in your handbag; there's no chance to fiddle with your major luggage after it's packed away.

Shall I Take the Children?

Well, why not take them? THEY love it and are usually as good as gold. How old do youngsters have to be to fly? Well, one young mother took her 12-day old son with her and said the trip was "just a good nap for the baby. "You can stow the little darlings into a plane and as soon as you've started, you're practically there.... United's stewardess-nurses provide the food the youngsters need and amuse them enroute.

How Does it Feel to Fly?

There is no sensation of great speed in a United plane even though your trip is unbelievably fast. The country seemingly unrolls smoothly, slowly under you. Your pilots in their own compartment are kept constantly in touch with such mun-

dane affairs as the weather by radio telephone. A direct radio beam marks the airway course: beckoning lights point like giant fingers; you drift off to sleep feeling that you're touching shoulders with the stars!

Indeed, planes were guided by radio beams. Weather reports were phoned in from hotel and railroad agents in a haphazard fashion, and meteorologists were consulted to ascertain general weather conditions en route. With no radar, pilots and ground personnel had to rely on their eyes to "clear the area." Flying was still an uncomfortable affair, and the mode of transportation was often dangerous.

Stewardesses Inspire Public Confidence in Air Travel — and Products

In March 1937, *Life* magazine reported on "five crashes in as many weeks." The article noted "that public confidence, after all these crack ups and charges, is still as great as it is in air transport is due in no small measure to the air hostess whose cheery presence in the plane bolsters public morale."

Public confidence in flight attendants spilled over into the advertising arena, too. Pretty professionals started to be featured to promote products. "382 Hours in the Air...on the Ground in 1 Pair of Silk Stockings!" boasted one 1935 ad testimonial from a United stewardess. "Air Line Stewardesses get amazing wear from sheer silk stockings washed daily with Ivory Flakes," the ad continued.

A

B

C

A

A quiet **tête-à-tête** over dinner in the late 1930s, the golden age of air travel. Credit: "Used by permission from American Airlines, Inc. American Airlines is a registered trademark of American Airlines, Inc."

B

Stewardesses were required to give a **military salute** to the captain upon his entering and leaving the plane. Credit: "Used by permission from American Airlines, Inc. American Airlines is a registered trademark of American

C

In just five years, in-flight food moved from a thermos of coffee and a leg of fried chicken to hot, three course meals served on china plates. Credit: "United Airlines Archives"

B-6297

"Scripto performance is no flight of fancy," said a smiling Eastern Air Lines flight attendant of "the pencil of the pro's."

Coca-Cola suggested in 1938 that you "Take off... Refreshed" and showed a beautiful stewardess sharing an ice-cold Coca-Cola with a handsome captain at the local airport soda fountain counter. It promised to make "travel more pleasant."

Air Hostesses Become Pop Culture Icons

By the mid 1930s, stewardesses had become full-fledged popular culture icons around the world. Movies like *Air Hostess* were launched with taglines that read, "She went up into the air for Romance and Thrills—Down to Earth for Love!" The story of *Air Hostess* is described as "the thrilling story of a girl of today who risked her heart and lost it above the clouds. Her romance side-slipped to a crack-up, then zoomed to a happy landing. It's swell entertainment."

Stories featuring the career highlights, opinions, and beauty secrets of the skygirls appeared in popular magazines. Books like *Jane, Stewardess of the Airways* featured stories of brave stewardesses pulling passengers from the wreckage of crashed planes. The women were admired for their professionalism, their beauty, and their heroism.

In 1936, a popular woman's magazine featured a romantic short story about a stewardess, underscoring again how strong a part of the national consciousness these women had become. There is tension when Copilot McDonald and Miss Gail Andrews, R.N., a beauty wearing "one of those jaunty overseas caps," first meet. "Heard the latest crack the mechanics have thought up?" he asks. "They call the crews Pilots, Mates and

Playmates...I think you'd make a swell playmate. You know, Gail, you're a honey. I could go for you." Gail does not respond to McDonald's line because she has her heart set on the pilot, Larry Hanson, who hates the idea of "putting women on a man's ship!"

Gail soon earns Hanson's respect, though, as she copes with the first-ever documentation of air rage. When a drunken passenger harasses her with inappropriate comments, Gail calls for the assistance of the armed copilot. The crazed passenger wrestles the gun out of his hand and knocks him out. The pilot — also armed with a Colt 38 — is then attacked and wounded but an athletic passenger subdues the threatening man and locks him in a bathroom. Gail then successfully lands the plane, causing the incapacitated pilot to conclude, "It's a good thing we have stewardesses on this airline."

Fares Drop, Passengers Increase

Passenger fares dropped from twelve cents per mile in 1926 to just under six cents per mile in 1935, a rate competitive with Pullman railroad fares. According to the Imperial Airways Chairman's Report in 1935, this was key to increasing traffic. "I can tell you that there is far greater pressure on us to reduce our fares and rates than to increase our speed," he said. "However, thanks to aeronautical science, we will achieve substantially higher speeds with our new fleet without increasing the cost of operation."

International routes were also opening up. In 1935, Imperial Airways and Qantas Empire Airways Limited cooperated to link services from London to Singapore to Australia. In 1936, the founder of Pan Am saw six rivals for global domination of the air routes: Aeroflot, Air France, Imperial Airways, Japan Airlines, KLM, and Luft Hansa. These airlines controlled routes through a combination of empire or regional strength, and could deny landing and refueling rights inside their zones of influence to any competitor.

By the close of the 1930s, double-decker sleeper planes were flying coast-to-coast in fifteen hours as opposed to several days by rail. Pan Am's Clippers serving the Pacific carried 74 passengers and featured 40 sleeping cabins, a dining room, lounge, bar, and dressing rooms for both men and women. The tail area of the plane could be converted into a deluxe bridal suite. Although advertisements for sky sleepers featured pictures of attentive stewardesses tucking mothers and children into bed, the vast majority of air travelers were still businessmen and politicians.

And soon the war would change the face of flying and spotlight the contributions women would make in the world of aviation.

Ch 2

The 1940s

Patriotic Sky Girls and Fly Girls

All was peaceful on this **sleeper,**
but the world was about to change
as the U.S. entered World War II.
Credit: "United Airlines Archives"

After the attack on Pearl Harbor in December 1941, 176 out of the U.S. airlines' 341 planes were appropriated by the armed forces. They were either commandeered outright or operated by the army under contract. A third of the commercial airlines' personnel also joined the armed forces. The entry of the United States into World War II created a huge demand for nurses, and stewardesses (all registered nurses) were released to the war effort. Nursing qualifications — but not height and weight restrictions — were relaxed for the airlines' new recruits.

The War Priority System: Regulations for In-Flight Service

Suddenly, there were mountains of rules as to who could fly and when. Air travel was restricted to those with essential jobs. The federal government issued the following regulations, called the War Priority System for Passengers:

Priority One: *Passengers traveling under government orders of the Army, Navy or White House.*

Priority Two: *Ferry Command Pilots en route to ferry bases or military installations.*

Priority Three: *Military or civilians on war business.*

Priority Four: *Military on leave and military cargo.*

With only half of their pre-war airplane fleet and two-thirds of their men, the commercial airlines were asked to assume greatly increased burdens, especially transporting freight and mail.

In-flight wartime regulations were also imposed. Flight attendants were instructed to avoid discussion of military, political, racial, and religious matters and report all attempts at that kind of conversation to the pilot. They were also required to look for signs of sabotage within the cabin.

The 1942 Continental Air Lines Hostess Manual included the following regulations for in-flight service:

A. *Curtains drawn: Ramp, takeoff, landing... "Smoking" signs [can be used] as signals.*

B. *Lavatory door: Locked while on ground and 10 minutes after takeoff.*

C. *Blankets: Carried in overhead rack. Wrapped or tied. They, as well as pillows, should be examined for concealment of sabotage.*

D. *After passengers have left: Ash tray and surrounding vicinity should be inspected to see that passengers have left nothing that might damage aircraft or persons.*

E. *Any extra baggage, parcels, brief cases not checked in baggage compartment must be checked, listed, tagged under passenger seat.*

F. *Cameras: Tagged. Kept in locked compartment and returned to passenger for deplaning.*

G. *Conversation: Discreet. No military matters, war industries discussed.*

H. *Failure of cooperation reported to Captain: A report of details, name, address, flight number, date.*

There was good reason for all of these rules. On a flight into Santa Fe, New Mexico, one Continental hostess noticed a little old lady peeking out through the curtains — which had been drawn in compliance with

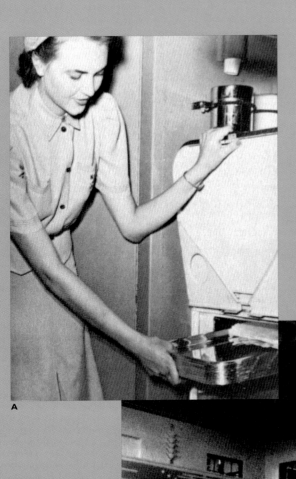

A

C

"Let me show you the way to go home!"

● There's no last minute rush, no regrets at leaving too soon—when you travel by Flagship! Take your time. Finish up your business in leisurely fashion (or tuck in another round of golf!) and then enjoy a quick, comfortable trip that lands you at home hours—even days—sooner. You save time at *both* ends of a Flagship journey!

American Airlines, Inc. serves the principal cities of the nation with frequent, convenient departures. Giant, luxurious Flagships. Delicious meals—included in your ticket. Stewardess service on all flights. For information about Flagship schedules and for reservations, call your Travel Agent or the nearest American Airlines office.

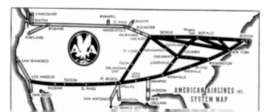

AMERICAN AIRLINES INC.
SYSTEM MAP

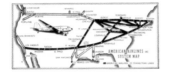

Uncle Sam travels by Air

HIS IS THE BIGGEST, busiest job in the nation. He has to be everywhere at once. And he hasn't a minute to waste. The time-saving efficiency which air transportation has given to business is magnified as it sets the pace of our national defense. The task is vital and air travel assures it will be accomplished . . . quickly!

AMERICAN AIRLINES *Inc.*

ROUTE OF THE FLAGSHIPS

B

WING YOUR WAY WITH . . . AUSTRALIAN NATIONAL AIRWAYS

A

In early 1941, the airlines were still competing with trains for the businessman's dollar. American promised that he would arrive **"hours or days"** earlier if he took the plane rather than the train. Credit: "Used by permission from American Airlines, Inc. American Airlines is a registered trademark of American Airlines, Inc."

B

In 1941, many stewardesses were released to the war effort and were replaced by **non-nurses.** Passengers changed, too, as the bulk of travelers were military personnel. Credit: "Used by permission from American Airlines, Inc. American Airlines is a registered trademark of American Airlines, Inc."

C

Australian National Airways adopted this military look for its air hostesses. Credit: "Australian National Airways."

war regulations — and had reprimanded the woman three times. The hostess dutifully filled out an irregularity report describing the incident. The FBI later informed the hostess that the little old lady was actually a spy in disguise who had been snapping photographs of the top secret military installation at Los Alamos!

Women Fly and Build Planes in WWII

Women's wartime contributions to aviation extended to both civilian and military activities. In June 1941, Jacqueline Cochran piloted a bomber to England as a Flight Captain in the British Air Transport Auxiliary (ATA). She helped organize a similar U.S. unit, the Women's Airforce Service Pilots (WASPs) soon thereafter, supplying more than one thousand auxiliary women pilots for the armed forces.

England's hero Amy Johnson was killed over the Thames estuary in 1941 on a mission to deliver an Airspeed Oxford airplane for the ATA. Countless other women pilots lost their lives in the line of duty serving their countries.

Throughout the war years, women contributed to the world of aviation by ferrying planes of all kinds across hostile territories and building airplanes in aircraft plants. After the war, however, women were not allowed to serve as pilots in the Air Force, nor were they hired as pilots for commercial airlines.

Uniforms mean uniformity. Here, a United staffer teaches new recruits how to pin a hat.
Credit: "United Airlines Archives"

A Women's Union

Because of the war, United and other major carriers hired non-nurse stewardesses known as "co-eds." Like the flying nurses, these young women could be dispatched to work at any time, day or night, and for unlimited hours. In 1944, former United stewardess Ada Brown organized almost 300 women to set up the world's first stewardess union. This allowed the women some ability to negotiate their wages and working conditions.

By 1943, the airlines were carrying twice as much cargo and mail as in peacetime and flying more passenger miles. The number of people flying had dropped by 25 percent, but travelers, predominantly on war business, were flying further on each trip.

Despite the circumstances, new airlines were cropping up and, with a shortage of men as personnel, female flight attendants became a necessity. Delta Air Lines began their first stewardess service in 1940; Continental Air Lines hired their first chief hostess the following year. Pan Am hired their first stewardess in 1944.

For women of the decade, a new professional opportunity had emerged. It was one of the few acceptable professions a woman could enjoy before "settling down to marriage."

Wings Before Rings; A Typical 1940s Stewardess

A United Air Lines' promotional/recruitment pamphlet described the average stewardess of the 1940s: "First of all, she has come to United from many other occupations — modeling, nursing, business or directly from college. On a more personal basis, Miss Average Stewardess is a comely five feet, five inches tall, has brown hair and brown eyes. Like most young career women, she likes sports, music and dancing for relaxation in off-duty hours. She likes to cook on her days off and her idea of a 'dream vacation' is more travel on the airways of the world. On an average, she will fly 25 months before undertaking the greater complexities of marriage."

Earning Her Wings

A five-week training course at the United Stewardess Center was required of each stewardess before she donned her blue uniform. "There she practices serving meals in full scale replicas of Mainliners' cabins and galleys, learns about infant care and how to aid mothers with small children, and how to answer questions on air routes, flight connections and geography. She also becomes familiar with such interesting subjects as the principles of aeronautics, aircraft types, meteorology and communications." After earning her silver wings upon graduation, the new stewardess was assigned to one of ten cities and paired with a senior stewardess who acted as her flying partner until she was allotted a regular schedule. Miss United still had to be over 21 "but not yet 27," five feet two inches tall, "but not over five feet seven" and weigh under 135 pounds.

Fast Service Complete with Genie

American Airlines had DC-6s and Convairs to fill as well. They announced the "5 mile-a-minute flagship fleet," speeding up airmail and air cargo and promised "more speed, more comfort, better service."

A

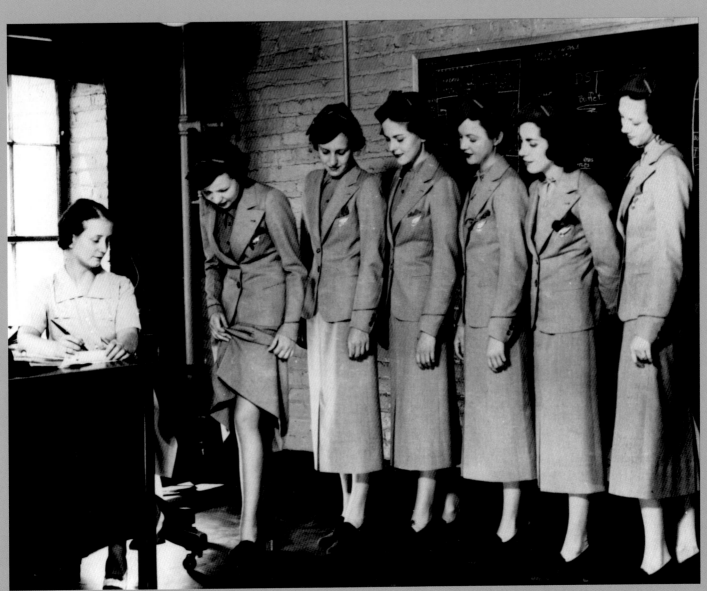

B

She adds FRIENDSHIP *to the Flagships!*

The Flagship stewardess personifies the friendly service for which American Airlines, Inc. is known.

Her gracious manner and thoughtful attention to her passengers add immeasurably to the comfort and the pleasure of their trip.

While making countless friends for our airline, she has won for herself an enviable place in air transportation. American is justly proud of the tradition of service our stewardesses have established on the Flagships.

ALL YEAR 'ROUND, TRAVEL IS BETTER BY AIR   BEST BY **AMERICAN AIRLINES** INC.

Typical Convair flight times were one hour from New York to Boston and three hours, fourteen minutes from Cleveland to Nashville. Larger windows, built-in boarding steps. larger overhead compartments, reclining seats and a club lounge were all features of the newer, larger planes. American also boasted "Your own Aladdin's Lamp. Press your button — and that pleasant Genie of the Airways — the American Airlines Stewardess — is at your side, preparing to serve you with magazines, writing paper, a pillow for napping." And, of course, the stewardess had to look pretty while performing her duties.

The Diaper Special

Throughout the 1940s, the male business traveler was every airline's main customer. In 1946, in an effort to expand its consumer base, United began a daily Nursery Liner Service. The flight, known as The Diaper Special, was devoted to mother and baby passengers flying between San Francisco and Los Angeles. Baby food, disposable diapers, rattles, dolls, and teddy bears crowded the twin-engine DC-3 for this special flight. The Diaper Special was not well subscribed, however, and the service only lasted three months.

B

Fabric Restrictions Meant Shorter Skirts

The war years had an unexpected influence on fashion. Hostesses' uniforms had become shorter and tighter, reflecting the L-85 ruling, a wartime regulation which restricted the yardage of fabric that could go into skirts, blouses, dresses, jackets, and coats. Like the Hollywood movie stars, flight attendants became pin-up girls celebrated for their beauty. The newly launched Continental Air Lines hired a Hollywood makeup artist to instruct stewardesses on how to achieve the film star look.

Pretty Noses and Fresh Breath

In the U.S., the advertising community seized the opportunity and soon images of smiling stewardesses were used to promote products in categories from stockings to toothpaste. The blitz of ads covered a plethora of themes from the "patriotism and product" ads showing hostesses supporting the war effort while promoting products, to in-flight encounters leading to true love.

"Pilots love pretty noses," reads an ad for Du Barry Beauty Preparations, a makeup line. "American Airlines Flight No. 7 to Chicago is ready on the runway. Cargo aboard; passengers checked; door locked tight on the silvery-slim ship. But not until ramp agent Betty Beach puts her finger on her pretty little nose does the pilot know what he wants to know most of all; that he's ready to roll and leaving on schedule." An artist's rendering of a smiling young woman in uniform touching her nose is the visual.

A famous mint company promised "Love at First Flight" and related the story of a blossoming romance aloft, facilitated by an air hostess. "I was practically head-over-heels from the minute we took off at Tulsa. But, shucks, how could I stand a chance with a movie gal?" the hero laments. "What a break for me when she signaled the hostess and said something about her mouth feeling dry and parched like…I almost sprained my wrist getting my pack of Life Savers across the aisle…But she smiled as she took one and the first thing you know, we were talking away at a great rate."

c

Glamour Girls Discuss the Perfect Man

In the public eye, a stewardess' life had glamorous cachet, and the media often treated them like movie stars.

Suddenly, the world was interested in stewardesses' opinions on everything from beauty products to qualities of the perfect man. In 1949, United Air Lines' stewardesses took part in a survey polling the traits of an ideal husband, and the findings were released to an interested public via a national news bureau. "The young lady of today thinks the muscle man is passé and that wavy brown hair, blue eyes, pipe smoking, and a distinct fondness for children are marks of an ideal husband," the press release states.

"The perfect man should be taller than the girl, but he need be built only in such proportions that his suits — gabardine preferably — don't hang like potato sacks." The attendants agreed that marrying for love instead of money was best, and that they did not like mustaches.

"Understanding, honesty, good disposition" were the top three character traits of the ideal man. Conceit was the predominant pet peeve, while "taking the fairer sex for granted" and "being late for dates" tied as second. "What burns me," related one stewardess, "is having a fellow make a date and then when he arrives, he asks, 'Now what shall we do?'"

Bombers Converted to Passenger Planes

After the war, airplane manufacturers amended their bomber designs to produce planes that carried 80 passengers. Filling them was a challenge as people still rode trains and now drove automobiles in preference to flying. But as bigger and more comfortable planes were designed and built, the airlines lured more passengers aboard and the industry continued to grow.

A

East or West — the Clipper way's best!

Club lounge downstairs is a congenial spot to meet people, enjoy refreshments. Only the spacious "double-deckers" offer this extra luxury . . . and so much room to roam around!

Bermuda's autumn weather is delightful! There's pleasure for every taste, every budget. Excellent hotels, coral beaches, sailing, deep-sea fishing, golf, tennis. Round trip from New York to smart America-class Clipper is only $126 plus tax.

Hawaii is nearer than ever by double-decked Clipper! Sun-warmed breezes lure you outdoors for sports. Gay social life in the evening. Round trip from California, $288 plus tax.

Only Pan American flies giant DOUBLE DECKED Clippers to both Bermuda and Hawaii!

No extra fare to go the fastest way . . . the most luxurious way! Only Pan American flies double-decked "America"-class Clippers to Bermuda from New York in less than 3 hours . . . to Hawaii from San Francisco in 8½ hours, from Los Angeles in 9½.

No other type of airliner is so quiet in flight . . . so smooth and steady. You'll find specially designed lounge seats, scores of other improvements! Only $25 extra for an extra-large, foam-soft berth to Hawaii (when two occupy it, $12.50 each).

Other luxury Clippers fly to Hawaii from Seattle and Portland . . . to Bermuda from Boston. For fares and reservations, call your Travel Agent or Pan American.

PAN AMERICAN
World's Most Experienced Airline

B

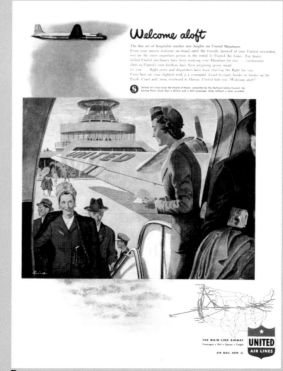

Welcome aloft

The fine art of hospitality reaches new heights on United Mainliners. From your instant welcome on board until the friendly farewell of your United stewardess, you are the most important person in the world to United Air Lines. For hours, skilled United mechanics have been readying your Mainliner for you . . . continental chefs in United's own kitchens have been preparing savory meals for you . . . flight crews and dispatchers have been charting the flight for you. From here on, your slightest wish is a command. Coast to coast, border to border on the Pacific Coast and, soon, westward to Hawaii, United bids you "Welcome aloft!"

United Air Lines holds the Award of Honor, presented by the National Safety Council, for having flown more than a billion and a half passenger-miles without a fatal accident.

THE MAIN LINE AIRWAY
Passengers • Mail • Express • Freight

AIR MAIL NOW 5¢

UNITED AIR LINES

D

LONDON will be host to the '48 Olympic Games this summer. Plan now to stop over and see them! From London, eastward, Pan American offers daily service to Brussels, Frankfurt, Prague, Vienna. Also regular flights to Istanbul, India, and around-the-world.

PARIS in June is something to remember! The great city is accessible on the Pan American World Airways System from either London or Lisbon (see map below) . . . Or, 75 minutes by connecting airline, from Brussels. Fare from New York (via London) $370.

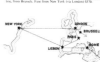

BY THE ROUTES shown above, Pan American offers the fastest service to both London and Lisbon. Other lines show routes of the Pan American System on the continent of Europe. FARES from New York (subject to change): London $370. Lisbon $376. Extra charge for berths.

Finest and Fastest Service to Europe

ONLY PAN AMERICAN OFFERS the luxury of non-stop sleeper service from New York to London! Four-engine Constellation-type Clippers fly you smoothly and swiftly "above the weather" . . . have comfortable reclining seats as well as roomy, bed-size berths.

LONDON, BY FLYING CLIPPER, is now only a good night's sleep away from New York! You step aboard a big 4-engine Constellation early in the evening . . . sleep in a big, wide, full-size berth as you fly non-stop to the British Isles . . . and arrive, rested and refreshed, in time for lunch the very next day!

This new luxury service to London is offered only by Pan American. The Flying Clippers lead the way, too, with the fastest service to Lisbon. And from either London or Lisbon (see map) you can continue on to Paris by the 4-engine Constellations of the Pan American System.

Make your Flying Clipper reservations to Europe now. Call your Travel Agent or the nearest Pan American office.

NEW YORK TO **LONDON** NON-STOP 13¾ HOURS
NEW YORK TO **LISBON** ONE-STOP 13½ HOURS

PAN AMERICAN WORLD AIRWAYS

SYSTEM OF THE FLYING CLIPPERS · WORLD'S MOST EXPERIENCED AIRLINE

C

Best bill of fare in the air

Go ahead, feast your eyes . . . and wish you were on a TWA Skyliner! Food like this makes dining with TWA a different, delightful interlude and one of the high spots of your Constellation flight. It's fun being TWA's guest because there's no standing in line, no tipping and no check. You stay right in your comfortable seat, and a whole wonderful meal like this is brought to you with TWA's compliments, on all regular-fare flights at mealtime.

Where in the world do **you** want to go? For information and reservations, call TWA or see your travel agent.

Fly the finest... **FLY TWA**

TRANS WORLD AIRLINES
U.S.A. · EUROPE · AFRICA · ASIA

Ch 3

The 1950s

The Stewardess as a Wife-in-Training

1952

LEAP YEAR

The **"wings or rings"** dilemma continued through the 1950s, as women had to be single to fly. Stewardesses typically flew for less than two years before getting married. Credit: "United Airlines Archives"

y 1951, there were 3,400 stewardesses in U.S. skies. Although many airlines had their own stewardess training programs, there still were a number of training schools which had cropped up across the country to cash in on the hopes and dreams of sky girl hopefuls. In addition to the usual aspects of in-flight service, attendants were taught the requisites of good conversation. A typical 1950s training book suggests that the perfect stewardess should combine the authority of a drill sergeant, the comforting qualities of a mother, and the subservient, flirtatious attentions of a geisha, with the facts and conversation of a tour guide:

1. *Be a good, sincere listener. Ask leading questions and show interest in conversation. This allows the passenger the feeling of importance.*

2. *Avoid talking about yourself and encourage passengers to talk about themselves. This procedure will make their trip pleasant.*

3. *Avoid argumentation. There should be no occasion for a Stewardess to participate in an argument on board an airplane. Nothing can be gained by argument for opinions are rarely changed by this type of conversation. The aim of Stewardess work is to please passengers. Argument creates opposition and disgust and will not please, there fore defeating the aim of stewardess work.*

4. *Avoid flippant or smart answers regardless of how foolish or irrelevant questions may be.*

5. *Avoid any type of conversation which is unladylike.*

6. *Avoid lengthy conversations. Generally, short, concise conversations will be more effective.*

7. *Information concerning air transportation shall be presented in as clear and interesting a manner as possible. This information shall be given at every opportunity but shall not be forced on passengers. Passengers should be allowed to ask questions as indicative of their interests.*

In 1952, the U.S. Civil Air Administration required all flight attendants on commercial aircraft to be cabin safety professionals, thoroughly trained in in-flight safety procedures.

U.S. Stewardesses Reflect the "Perfect Wife"

Despite the fact that women had been instrumental in the war effort and proved their competence on land and in the air, social norms in the 1950s shifted again, sending women back into the home. By the early part of the decade, returning GIs had gained an education, a job, a wife, and a family. Affordable housing was growing by leaps and bounds, and a "little woman," adept at the home arts of cooking, cleaning, child-raising, and socializing, was the new ideal. There were exceptions to the rule. In 1953, aviation pioneer Jacqueline Cochran, piloting an F-86, became the first woman to break the sound barrier. That same year, she set several world speed records. Stewardesses, however, reflected the image of "the perfect wife." They wore shapely but demure uniforms and were shown in advertisements to be as adept at warming a baby's bottle as mixing a martini.

Bobby Pins and Cigarettes; Stewardesses Promote More Products

Celebrity endorsements, the mainstay of marketing executives in the 1950s, soon featured stewardesses. Flamingo Products invited women to "set your hair with the Official Bob Pins of American Airlines Stewardesses," and a smiling stewardess is quoted:

Super Service at your command

All the time — All the way wherever you fly with Australia's International Airline!

The customer is always *right* — **with Qantas!** Constant care for personal comfort makes *all* the difference, all the way — day or night. To Qantas all-Australian crews, unsurpassed in long distance flying experience, *it's always a pleasure*, as well as a *duty*, to be of service — to every passenger.

Fast, frequent Qantas services, covering more than 38,000 miles of unduplicated air routes, link Australia with Indonesia, Malaya, Ceylon, India, Pakistan, Lebanon, Europe, Philippines, Japan, Hong Kong, and over 70 points in New Guinea and the South-West Pacific Islands. *For trip-planning help, consult your travel agent.*

FLY QANTAS — *There's a World of Difference*

A

C

B

A

A

Two American Airlines stewardesses **modeling the summer and winter uniforms.** Credit: "Courtesy of the American Airlines C.R. Smith Museum"

B

For the hostesses at Scandinavian Airlines Systems (SAS), uniforms by Christian Dior reflected the **"New Look,"** which revolutionized fashions in Europe. Credit: "Courtesy Scandinavian Airlines System (SAS)"

C

First class passengers were served sake and Japanese food by a **kimono-clad hostess** and treated to traditional music on Japan Airlines. Credit: "Courtesy Japan Airlines"

"Our high neatness standards demand perfectly groomed hair." Celanese Corporation of America promised "You will like fabrics made of Acetate for the same reasons air-hostesses do!" Wrinkle recovery and easy laundering are two reasons cited for those "living out of a suitcase." "It's wise to smoke extra-mild Fatima," says one ad featuring a beautiful Northwest stewardess whose caption reads simply, "I agree." Sometimes celebrities of the fledgling television industry appeared aloft with stewardesses for a double whammy endorsement.

Recruiting the Ideal Candidate

For almost 20 years, the industry had been refining rules for the sky girls. A 1953 summary of the recruiting rules for the various carriers dictated that young women who were candidates for stewardesses be:

• Between 5'2" and 5'7" tall.
• Have a good figure, weighing between 100 and 125 lbs, with weight proportionate to height.
• Between 20 and 26 years old.
• Single with no dependents (marriage terminates employment).
• Charming and personable with poise and beauty.
• Be in perfect physical condition with even, white teeth, clear white skin without blemishes, straight, slender legs and attractive, shiny hair.
• Willing to retire between ages 30 and 32.

A

B

C

The applicant was asked to send two recent photographs along with her application form — one head and shoulders, one full figure — in hopes of impressing the personnel man. Because, for airlines, choosing the right "girl" was still man's work.

Of Gloves and Girdles; Keeping Up Appearances

Once flying, the stewardess had to keep up appearances. Most airlines had a mirror on the hostesses' lounge wall beside which was mounted a checklist asking:

Stewardess, is your...

- Smile friendly and sincere?
- Posture erect and poised?
- Makeup neat and natural?
- Nails manicured and polished?
- Ribbon new and trimmed?
- Gloves white and tailored?
- Uniform cleaned and pressed?
- Purse orderly and polished?
- Shoes repaired and shined?
- Insignia on?
- Hair short and styled?
- Hose seams straight?
- Slip not showing?

D

A
The newly revitalized **Japan Airlines** offered a classic Western look while greeting passengers outside the plane. Credit: "Courtesy Japan Airlines"

B
Inside the **PSA cabin,** flight attendants prepared drinks while passengers chatted in a roomy lounge, an unusual feature for intrastate flights. Credit: "Photo courtesy of US Airways Group"

C
Swissair, who hired the first European stewardess in 1934, focused on their **female cabin crew** in a series of print advertisements. Credit: "SAir Group Photo Library"

D

E

Many airlines insisted that their female employees wear a girdle at all times. The supervisors could check compliance by giving the stewardesses a quick pat on the bottom when they went on duty. A supervisor report form had to be filled out for each flight with comments to be made on attendants' attitude, appearance and uniform. Airlines had "appearance counselors" to help set standards and "appearance rooms" featured weigh scales. Small hats, high heels, gloves, and girdles characterized the fashion of the decade.

Real Men Fly the Executive: Babies Ride Mainliners

United established their men-only Executive service in 1953, operating between Chicago and New York. The only women allowed aboard the DC-6 Mainliner were the stewardesses. The Executive service flew 10,500 segments with a load factor of 80 to 90 percent during its 17 years of operation.

Some Mainliners made concessions to the women, as well, with complete service for baby. One advertisement promises, "after you board your Mainliner the stewardess will relieve you of miscellaneous packages and diaper bags. She will then assist you to select the best seat available for comfort and privacy...." The Mainliner Baby Kit, a boxed collection of crackers, baby powder, diapers, and other essentials, as well as a bottle cooler for children's milk, was offered to mothers free of charge.

A Smoke, a Drink, a Game of Cards: Lounging in the Lounges

Socializing in the air was a major feature of postwar air travel. Stewardesses encouraged passengers to play cards or meet one another for drinks and a smoke. Many of the world's leading airlines — including Qantas, Thai Airways International (THAI), Air France, and KLM —

were using Lockheed Super Constellations, known as Connies, while giants like British Overseas Airways Corporation had a fleet of Stratocruisers — big, luxurious, double-decker planes which were quieter and faster than former models.

More and more exotic décor, elaborate meals, and extensive in-flight service were used to entice passengers and differentiate the airlines. Most airlines featured lounges sporting interesting themes to spark the imagination of travelers. BOAC's Monarch service, an overnight sleeper from London to New York, offered passengers a seven-course dinner with cocktails, private sleeping berths, and a lower deck lounge in which to meet fellow travelers. TWA had its glamorous dining room, and United its Red Carpet Room. In 1955, Northwest introduced its Fujiyama Room, a lounge in the lower level of a Stratocruiser decked out in Asian splendor "symbolizing the other lands we serve beyond the Pacific. When you step down the stairway from the main deck of the NWA Stratocruiser into the Fujiyama Room, you enter another world, tasting the charm of the Orient," the ad continues. "Here you will enjoy delicacies from our Fujiyama tray. Cocktail service too. At tea time, Oriental jasmine tea. And such meals — juicy steaks, ocean-fresh seafood salads...."

Many European airlines had similar in-flight draws. Lufthansa celebrated Oktoberfest aloft with stewardesses in Dirndl dresses serving mugs of local beer tapped from a keg. Stewards mixed drinks for passengers in coach, while a chef prepared traditional German meals in situ for the First Class passengers.

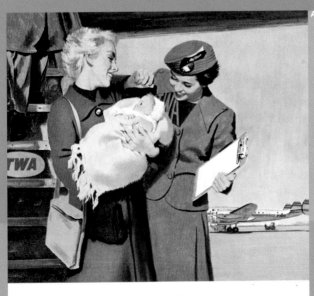

A

The RIGHT formula for traveling with a baby

We get praised to the skies by mothers traveling with small children. And kind of like it, too. For, if there's one thing a TWA Skyliner can do... it's give a young mother's morale a big lift when there's a long journey ahead. No more restless, weary tots. Five-mile-a-minute speed sees to that. And when baby is not sleeping like a kitten on a cloud, a thoughtful TWA hostess helps you keep him on schedule while we keep on ours.

Where in the world do you want to go? For information and reservations, call TWA or see your travel agent.

ACROSS THE U.S. AND OVERSEAS...YOU CAN DEPEND ON

TWA
TRANS WORLD AIRLINES
U.S.A. EUROPE·AFRICA·ASIA

Where on earth could you find such service ?

You feel genuine friendliness when a TWA hostess smiles "hello," and sense relaxation as soon as you settle in your TWA Constellation seat. Thoughtful planning shortens your journey. Guest-of-honor attention anticipates your needs, caters to every wish and satisfies your new-found appetite with a meal you'll talk about for days! Yes, you'll like your trip by TWA Constellation. Where on earth could you find such service?

Where in the world do you want to go? For information and reservations, call TWA or see your travel agent.

ACROSS THE U.S. AND OVERSEAS...YOU CAN DEPEND ON

TWA
TRANS WORLD AIRLINES
U.S.A. EUROPE·AFRICA·ASIA

NOW! TWA TRANSATLANTIC SKY TOURIST CONSTELLATIONS FROM NEW YORK TO: LONDON $270 — PARIS $290 — FRANKFURT $313.10 — ZURICH $313.10 — ROME $357.20

B

A

B

A

California carrier Pacific Southwest Airlines (PSA) recognized early that **stewardesses were a key component** of their image, as is apparent from their elegant uniforms. Credit: "Photo courtesy of US Airways Group"

B

American's ticket envelope featured an artist's rendering of the **ideal stewardess.** Credit: "Used by permission from American Airlines, Inc. American Airlines is a registered trademark of American Airlines, Inc."

60

Welcoming in the Jet Era

The British-made and designed de Havilland Comet was the world's first commercial jet plane. It traveled distances in half the time of propeller planes and was popular in Europe. Then a series of crashes due to a phenomenon called "metal fatigue" effectively grounded the Comet.

In October, 1958, Pan Am inaugurated Boeing 707 service between New York and Paris, ushering in the U.S. vision of the jet age. Soon, 707s were the new favorites of the fleets. The ride was quiet and smooth compared to propeller-driven planes. It was also much faster than its predecessors; American Airlines did the trip from Los Angeles to New York in five and a half hours! Comfort was another popular feature of the 707. Continental's Gold Carpet Service linking Chicago, Los Angeles, Denver, and Kansas City promised, "You'll sip champagne and watch TV enjoying two spacious lounges." Vintage wines, roast breast of game bird, pastries, and liqueurs were part of the new gourmet menus.

Exotic Perquisites for Stewardesses

With so much luxury aloft and so many opportunities to see the world, no wonder stewardesses had become known as glamour girls. They shopped for leather goods in Italy, watched native dancers perform in Thailand, picked up handcrafted bargains in Java and Bali, and brought fresh pineapples from Hawaii back to their friends and family during the icy mainland winters. They dined in the best restaurants in Tokyo and Sydney and discovered the back-street delicacies of various Caribbean islands. They could be seeing the sights of New York City one day and frolicking in the Pacific surf the next...until marriage ended their careers, that is.

Many Miles, Many Meals Served Before Marriage

According to a 1958 article in *Life* magazine, most stewardesses resigned from their career inside of two years to get married. In those two years on the line, the average hostess was in the air some 1,900 hours and on duty on the ground another 1,100, having helped 15,000 passengers and served 8,000 meals. The average stewardess would have made 3,500 take-offs and landings and flown 600,000 miles before the wedding bells rang.

As the sedate fifties gave way to the swinging sixties, a flight attendant's experience aloft — as well as the public's perception of the stewardess — would soon change dramatically.

c

c
The American Airlines Stewardess College was hailed as
"the first and only" of its kind, and featured training areas,
dormitories, pools, and a gymnasium. Credit: "Used by
permission from American Airlines, Inc. American Airlines
is a registered trademark of American Airlines, Inc."

A

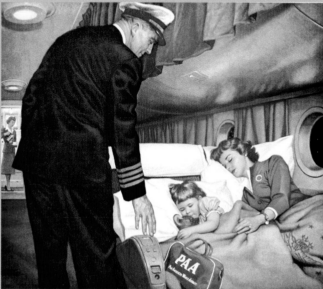

A

This 1959 **Russian magazine** cover shows
a group of Aeroflot stewardesses leaving their
latest airliner. Aeroflot was one of the world's
largest airlines. Credit: "Aeroflot"

B

A pretty stewardess shared **top billing** with the
cities covered by the airline in this United ad.
Credit: "United Airlines Archives"

C

Australian bathing beauties beckoned U.K.
businessmen when Qantas and BOAC teamed up.
Credit: "This photograph has been reproduced
courtesy of Qantas Airways Limited"

D

Life magazine pictured hostesses from 53 airlines that flew out of New York and their vast

array of outfits. Some airlines differentiated themselves with uniforms based on their traditional

local or national costumes. Credit: "PeterStackpole/TimePix © 1958 Time Inc. Reprinted by permission"

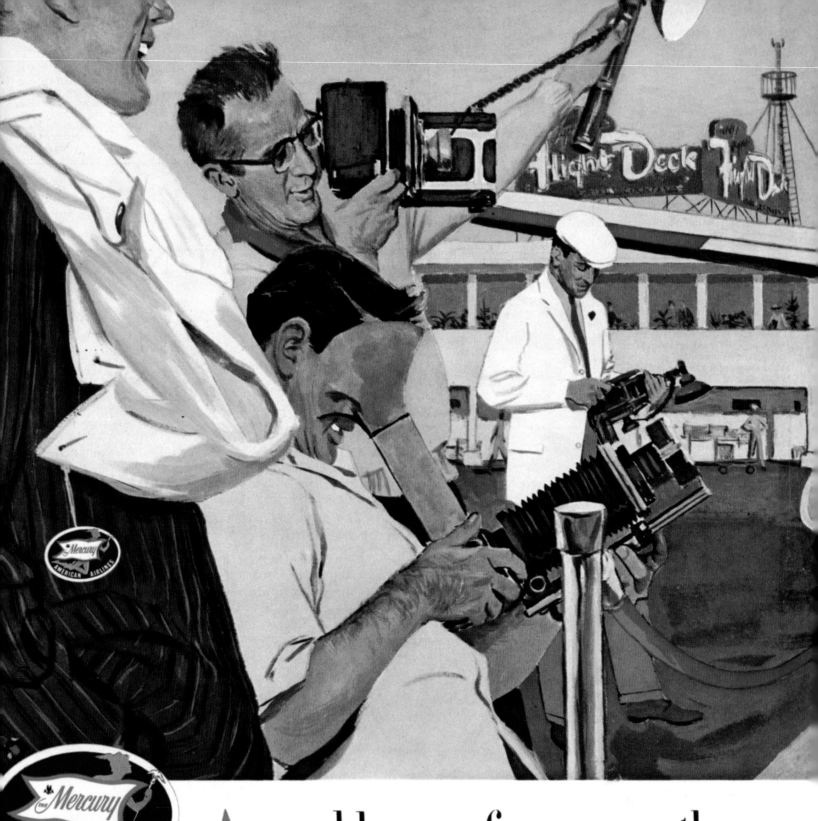

An emblem as famous as the peo

At the airport, the day's most important travelers will most frequently embark on American's DC·7 Mercury. The fame of the Mercury owes much to the distinction of its passengers who have established it as the luxury leader in the world of flight.

Everything aboard the Mercury merits this ac claim. The deluxe cabin is spacious; all seats are reserved; there is an attractive lounge. You fly th DC·7, America's fastest airliner. The Mercur menu is prepared with lavish care and the fa

AMERICAN AIRLINES

AIR TRAVEL IS AMERICA'S BEST BARGAIN

Since 1941, the index of retail prices for other products has risen almost 85%, while the total increase in the cost of air transportation, despite constantly improving service, has been less than 4%.

Another celebrity departs on the Mercury from Los Angeles International Airport

it serves – The Mercury

d Mercury service anticipates your every wish. magnificent Mercury represents the highest lard in luxury travel as well as the superior ce you find all through the Flagship Fleet. American—America's leading airline.

AMERICAN AIRLINES
America's Leading Airline

A

B

C

You get all these advantages
only on the World's Most Experienced Airline

- ☑ The most overseas flying experience—by far.
- ☑ Giant double-decked "Strato" Clippers . . . new 300 m.p.h. Super-6 Clippers.
- ☑ Berths available to most cities . . . bed-length Sleeperette service to many.
- ☑ Flights to every continent and around the world. One ticket takes you all the way! Helpful offices in 411 cities across the globe.
- ☑ The most frequent flights—and at the most convenient hours.

More people fly overseas by *PAN AMERICAN*

D

E

D

Pan Am served meals by **Maxim's of Paris**, and offered lower deck lounges and sleeping berths on their flights to Europe. Credit: "Pan American Airways"

E

A pair of stewardesses chatted with a child on a cobblestone street in Puerto Rico, the kind of exotic destination that was all in a **day's work for the air hostess.** Credit: "Joe Scherschel/TimePix ©1958 Time Inc. Reprinted by permission"

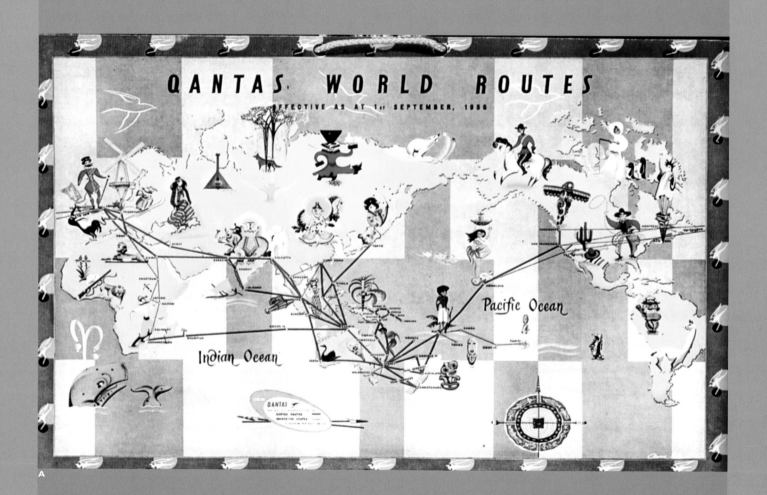

A

B

C

Ch 4

The 1960s
Stewardesses Become Sex Objects

Aloft, **Qantas** air hostesses wore a simple dress, hat, and a big smile. Credit: "This photograph has been reproduced courtesy of Qantas Airways Limited"

The decade opened with Boeing 707s and their jet rivals providing the major airlines with direct service between the world's great cities. Flights between major cities were accomplished in record-breaking times; crossing the Atlantic from New York to Paris took less than six hours. The cigar tube-shaped planes were fast, but gone were the sleeper berths and cocktail lounges of the 1950s. Gone, too, were the luxurious lounges where passengers whiled the hours away sipping cocktails and chatting with fellow travelers. The new, smaller, faster planes meant that flight attendants had less time to accomplish their in-flight duties, but more interesting international destinations to visit on layovers.

In social terms, the 1960s were nothing like the 1950s. If the archetypal western woman of the 1950s was a wife and mother, her counterpart in the 1960s was free-spirited and independent, took the Pill, and liked being single. The sexual revolution had arrived.

Shorter Flight Times, Shorter Skirts

Throughout the world beautiful, young women became marketing tools used by the airlines (and virtually every other industry) to promote their services. Because the international carriers were flying the same type of plane to the same destinations, competition heated up. The new 707 design had sacrificed lounges to provide more revenue-generating seats; marketing based on comfort and luxury disappeared. The airlines focused on their flight attendants. In print and on television, sexually charged or innuendo-laden advertising was launched, all themed around the attractiveness of their female cabin crew.

Stewardesses became the product used to sell the airline and were repackaged, that is, dressed in alluring new ways. For decades, flight attendant's uniforms had reflected the public's general design trends. In the 1960s, flight attendant's outfits began to set the trends. Internationally-renowned designers were hired to outfit the women. Makeup and hair styles went mod. Psychedelic colors, clingy, man-made fabrics, false eyelashes, hot pants, and micro-minis were the order of the day.

"The End of the Plain Plane" and the Start of "The Air Strip"

In 1965, Mary Wells, an advertising executive based in New York City, came up with two back-to-back campaigns that best define the decade. Her client, Braniff Airlines, was a Dallas-based carrier that wanted to expand its presence to compete in the international arena. Wells' concept was to enhance the flying experience (and revenues) by incorporating art and fashion into it. A renowned designer was recruited to decorate the planes with bold motifs, creating tremendous, airborne works of art. Wells called it "the end of the plain plane." Braniff terminals were also redesigned with mirrored ceilings and funky furniture to resemble a groovy bachelor pad.

Emilio Pucci was hired to create an innovative uniform for the Braniff stewardesses the same year. The colorful, multi-layered costume was topped with a plastic, space-helmet/bubble-hat. Wells developed a campaign called "The Air Strip" which had flight attendants peeling off one or two garments per city like an airborne game of strip poker. Costume changes continued through the flight until the flight attendants had stripped down to a top and culottes.

Our whole new look,
is from the book
that gave the nineties glory—
From stem to stern,
from the century's turn,
It's like a Gold Rush picture story.

You'll enjoy the dress,
of each stewardess
as she pampers you with care—
their costumes flow,
from head to toe,
with an 1890 flair.

Add this and more,
to the speed in store
streaking northward through the heavens—
Alaska bound
near the speed of sound
In our Seven Twenty Sevens.

Alaska is just one easy day away from even the furthest point in the nation. Our Golden Nugget fan jets put you in Alaska even before you're there! Ankle deep, red pile carpeting — big tufted velvet seats — red velvet drapes with gold braid and tassels adorn the Gold Rush 'Gay 90's' interior. The tinkly ragtime music, the rhymed departure, arrival and inflight announcements and even the flight numbers 1898 and 1899 roll back the clock to the turn of the century.

GOLDEN NUGGET JETS

B

A

C

A

In Australia, this Ansett air hostess demonstrated the
freedom of movement achieved by the new uniform.
Credit: "Photo Courtesy Ansett Australia"

B

Taiwan-based China Airlines was emerging as
a player in the East. Here, air hostesses are
dressed in a variant of traditional costume.
Credit: "Courtesy China Airlines"

C

At American Airlines, the decade started with this
classic look. Credit: "Courtesy of the American
Airlines C. R. Smith Museum"

D

E

A

This **Carven-clad Scandinavian hostess** welcomed
passengers aboard an SAS flight. Credit: "Courtesy
Scandinavian Airlines System (SAS)"

The Air Strip was a huge success. Print ads swamped magazines and TV commercials featured a flight attendant stripping to the rhythmic beating of drums. The majority of the public loved it. They Air The Air Strip was a huge success. Print ads swamped magazines, and TV commercials featured a flight attendant stripping to the rhythmic beating of drums.

The majority of the public loved it. Reportedly, male fliers would call Braniff to see what they had missed by getting off the flight prior to the plane's final destination. Braniff stewardesses became the original trophy wives for wealthy Texas businessmen.

As Pucci was defining the Braniff stewardesses with his colorful designs, other designers were brought in. Pierre Cardin dressed the women of Pakistan International Airlines and United turned to Jean Louis of Hollywood fame. Pumps and less restrictive clothing were popular with the stewardesses of the mid 1960s; the girdles and gloves were off!

Of Paper Uniforms and Innuendo-Laden Ad Campaigns

Skirt lengths shortened, and sexist slogans grew as campaigns targeting male passengers were launched. In 1961, Continental initiated its "Proud Bird with the Golden Tail" campaign and dressed its stewardesses in gold uniforms. Later, Continental announced in print that, "we would move our tails for you." The double entendre led the airline to make a training film for their staff so that the flight attendants could respond to passengers' untoward remarks with appropriately witty comments.

WELCOME ABOARD

B·O·A·C

ROLLS-ROYCE 707

In 1968, TWA established a transcontinental Foreign Accents flight where the stewardesses' outfits as well as the cuisine, were designed to reflect each country served: lounge pajamas for New York, a French gold lamé cocktail dress, an English "serving wench" outfit and a Roman toga. The outfits were made of paper and flight attendants complained that male passengers burned holes in the outfits with their cigarettes as a joke. BOAC dressed flight attendants in paper dresses, as well, from London to the Caribbean. The dress came in a small, medium or large, and was packaged with scissors to cut the right length of hemline.

Stewardesses worldwide were judged by the same yardstick. Every major international carrier still insisted that the women had to be unmarried and, because they were single, much was made of their availability. United had a print campaign which featured the face of a pretty young woman in close-up. "Old Maid," the tagline ran, stating that the woman had been flying for two years without receiving a proposal of marriage. The friendly skies got a lot friendlier when the classic blue uniform was ditched for the "skimmer," a short, colorful dress fashioned from "pure virgin wool." TV campaigns mirrored print in their treatment of female flight staff. One Eastern Airlines commercial featured the voice-over of a man interviewing flight attendants and rejecting them one by one because they were not deemed sexually alluring enough for his airline. One Caribbean airline referred to its hostesses as "rare tropical birds" in a print campaign.

Asian Airlines Stress Hospitality

Traditional hospitality was the message from the Far East. Japan Airlines featured flight attendants dressed in traditional kimonos and promised to "introduce each passenger to the delights of Japanese comfort and hospitality." On China Airlines, hostesses wearing traditional cheong sam "pamper you…as you relax in an Oriental atmosphere." Air India promised "the exotic charm of Indian hospitality so graciously extended by fascinating sari-clad hostesses…."

Jealous Wives Reassured

Promotional and recruitment brochures reflected the attitude of the times as well as the airlines' various personalities. In a promotional pamphlet targeting women travelers called "Plane & Fancy," American Airlines answered a series of "women's questions" designed to

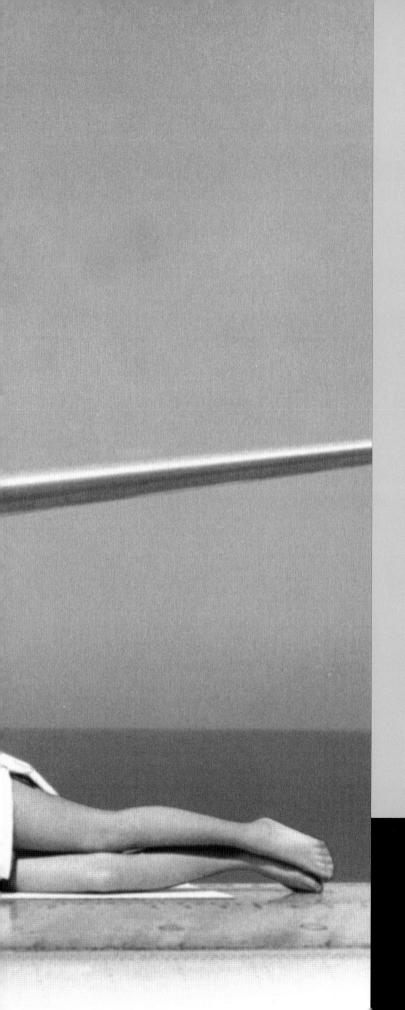

make flying more interesting to women. "Why Fly?" and "Tips for Women Travelling Alone" are tackled here along with "Packing Pointers" complete with hat, lingerie, and footwear suggestions. A section entitled "Do they really get all those proposals?" states that within two years, most American stewardesses leave their jobs to get married. "This isn't surprising," the text continues. "A girl who can smile for 5 hours is hard to find. Not to mention a wife who can remember what 124 people want for dinner...."

Jealous wives and girlfriends concerned that the flight attendants' charms might challenge the constancy of their mates were reassured, "Our jets fly so fast and the trip's so brief not even the American male is that fast and besides, our stewardesses are pretty busy taking care of all the passengers." The pamphlet concludes with the quality of education provided at American's Stewardess College and how the stewardesses will apply this knowledge for an average of 24 to 27 months before "the wedding bells will peal out and another lucky man carries off an AA stewardess."

Young, Healthy, and More Interesting

For over a decade, the three most coveted careers for young women in the U.S. remained actress, model, and stewardess. Despite its drawbacks, flying was still a relatively glamorous profession for beautiful young women.

Famed Hollywood designer Jean Louis designed the **Skimmer** for United, creating a style which was emulated by a number of airlines. Credit: "United Airlines Archives"

A
THAI hostesses model their new uniforms, designed by **Prince Kraisingh Vudhijaya.** Credit: "Courtesy THAI"

B
Before the friendly skies got so **crowded,** this United stewardess had time to keep score for the boys' card game. Credit: "United Airlines Archives"

C
Nationally-distributed *Parade* magazine noted how pretty stewardesses could increase ticket sales in their article on Pacific Southwest Airlines. Heart shaped hats and mini skirts accentuated the appeal of this California-based crew. Credit: "Reprinted with permission from Parade. Copyright © 1968 and courtesy Ms. Marva Shearer"

Parade

SEATTLE
Sunday Post-Intelligencer

COVER STORY:

GIRLS—THEY MAKE A LITTLE AIRLINE BIG
by Lloyd Shearer

CHINNING BEATS JOGGING
by Dr. Edwin F. Patton

c

A

Flight attendants handed out **board games** to amuse children on long flights. Credit: "Courtesy Omelock Collection"

B

A new network of TWA terminals in the early 1960s featured innovations like **carousel baggage delivery** and "instantaneous flight information." Credit: "Courtesy Omelock Collection"

C

A colorful **Air-India** timetable from 1966. Credit: "Courtesy Omelock Collection"

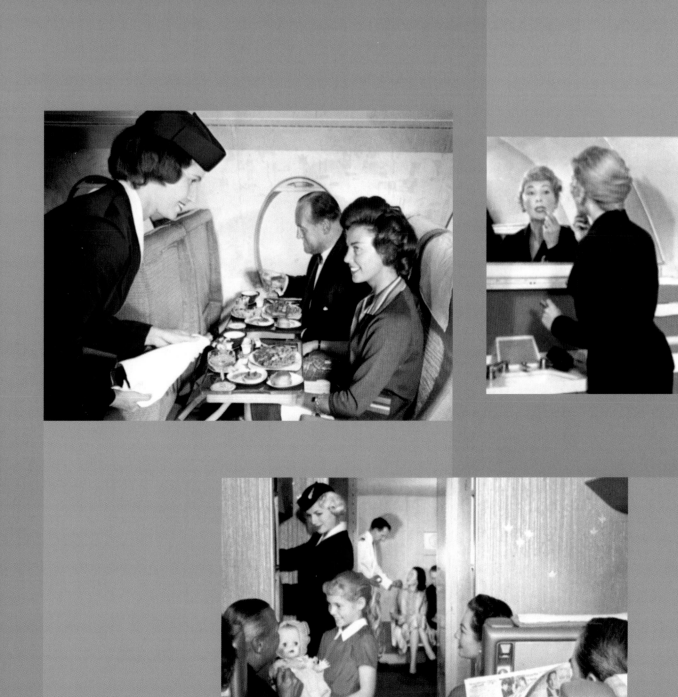

Trans-Canada Air Lines (TCA) advertised great food, great
service, and plenty of space — even a well-lighted powder
room for ladies — aboard their aircraft. Credit: "Durward
Cruickshank Archives"

Amidst the blitz of hot pants, innuendos, and strip-teases, Delta framed their flight attendants' appeal in a subtle way in a late 1960s in-flight promotional/recruiting brochure. "These fine young ladies are very special indeed…capable, sincere, friendly, well-poised…that's a Delta stewardess." Qualifications are listed thus: "Applicants must be between 20 thru 26 years of age, between 5'2" and 5'8", weight in proportion but not over 135 lbs., never married and in radiant good health." Delta's print campaigns, too, always imparted a respectful attitude about their cabin crew. "No floor show," read one ad, which showed a stewardess serving passengers in the cabin, "Just a working girl working."

United Airlines promised "A more interesting you" after the five-and-a-half-week course of studies at its Stewardess Center in Chicago was completed. "The new way you look, the interesting things you learn, the places you go, the people you meet all add up to a more interesting you! You gain invaluable experience that will be useful throughout the rest of your life…experience that is one of the best preparations for marriage or any other undertaking that a young woman can ever have."

Some conservative airlines, which didn't advertise the charm and availability of their flight attendants, focused on the charm and availability of the bikini-clad women their male passengers would meet at various destination points. Swissair ran a print campaign in 1962 featuring a bathing beauty on the beach and announcing "Lisbon is the place. Winter's not invited here. You will not soon hurry away."

WCA is going your way

Serving 60 cities in Washington, Oregon, Idaho, California, Utah, Montana, and Calgary in Canada.

WEST COAST AIRLINES

For information and reservations call WCA or your travel agent.

B

New, International Airlines Launched

Around the world, new airlines were cropping up. In 1961, THAI began operations with a Douglas DC-6B with 60 passengers and flew from Bangkok to Hong Kong. The airline was 70 percent government-owned and 30 percent SAS-owned. Prince Kraisingh Vudhijaya designed the traditional silk air hostesses' uniforms as well as the logo. In 1966, THAI became the first all-jet airline in Asia.

Beyond Hot Pants and Micro Minis

In the U.S., regional airlines were suddenly seeking ways to differentiate themselves in an over-crowded field. Aside from hot pants and short skirts, marketing ploys and in-flight theme concepts multiplied as local service airlines — with roughly 20 clearly-defined territories in the U.S. — sought to create an identity for themselves to an increasingly jaded public.

On the East Coast, Mohawk Airlines — founded in 1945 — was known as a small but successful upstate New York carrier. In 1960, Mohawk inaugurated its Gaslight Service which featured a Gay Nineties-style theme. DC-3s were decked out with gas lanterns, brocade curtains, and antimacassars on the seat backs; stewardesses in flowing satin gowns served passengers a snack and "a good five cent cigar."

PSA, a California-based airline which painted a smile under the nose of all of their planes, hired women who were celebrated for their beauty. PSA attendants wore the shortest, orange hot pants in the sky. The company made constant reference to the attractions of their flight crew, giving the women tongue-in-cheek buttons to wear that spelled out their view of what PSA stood for, "Pure, Sober and Available."

Flights of Fancy; Epic Poetry Aloft

In the Northwest, Alaska Airlines flights sported a Gold Rush theme with stewardesses dressed in 1890s style, floor length velvet skirts. The cabin, too, was decorated in the Gay Nineties theme. Passengers were welcomed aboard the "Golden Nugget jet" with rhymed in-flight announcements written in the style of 1890s epic poet, Robert Service. In part, flight attendants made the following announcements:

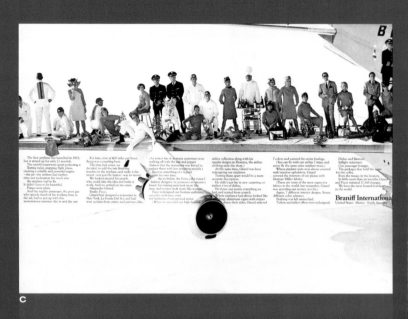

D

D

United's Skimmer was **less restrictive** than former
uniforms. The stewardesses reportedly loved it.
Credit: "United Airlines Archives"

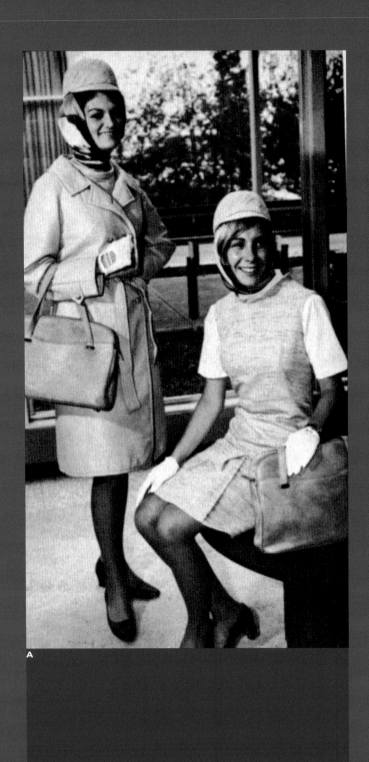

We're on our way to Nome today
Historic gold rush town
We'll announce the route and more to boot
And gently set you down.

Listen now for locations of the exit stations
There are seven by actual tally
There's a cabin door both aft and fore
And another in the galley.

Now if you'll raise your sight, there's a reading light
And air vents in each aisle
Or you can button press for the stewardess
For service with a smile.

We've lots to read and each baby need
And stationery, too.
So call on us, we love to fuss
Over every one of you.

Upon conclusion of the flight from Anchorage to Nome, Alaska Airlines' in-flight service concluded with the following verse:

Now a fond adieu to those of you
Who have to leave us here.
Please return once more to the fun in store
On the jet from yesteryear.

Food, too, was used to lure passengers aboard. In 1968, Pan Am announced that a famous Parisian restaurant was catering its flights. "Any time you're on a Pan Am Clipper, you're dining out with Maxim's of Paris…the same Maxim's that dreams up the finest international menu that ever got off the ground."

Take My Wife…Please

United developed a campaign called "Take Me Along" in 1967 aimed at wives to get their businessmen husbands to "take them along" on their trips. The campaign came complete with theme song, sheet music, and a print campaign offering reduced fares for wives so that a woman could "turn your husband's next business trip into a swinging time for both of you."

The Civil Rights Act Passes

In the midst of all of this activity, in 1964, the Civil Rights Act created new rules in the workplace. Employees could not be discriminated against because of age, sex, or race. Stewardesses even got a new name. They were to be called flight attendants. But they were far from being the respected professionals they had been in the past. Like most women in the workforce, flight attendants had fragmented or no union representation. The "don't marry, don't get pregnant" rules which had held sway for decades were now debatable under the new Civil Rights Act, but it would be years before these conventions were challenged in court. Appearance and weight issues were more problematic to challenge since some courts agreed that certain jobs for women required "looks."

No Knitting in View of Public for Australian Hostesses

In Australia, an Ansett-ANA Hostess Manual from 1965 advises that "The Company does not permit a Hostess to continue in this Department after Marriage," and warns that "the standard of appearance of our Hostesses is vitally important to Ansett-ANA. Hostesses who fail to maintain the standard must be prepared to accept correction and carry it out."

Miss Qantas!
And you'll miss a lot!

Only Qantas offers four great jetways to the world: the U.S.A. way, the Singapore way, the Hong Kong way, the Mexico way.

It's only with Qantas that you can fly right round the world without changing airlines, and only Qantas offers so many world jet flights a week, direct from Australia.

Only Qantas flies V-Jets, fastest in round-world service, and with Qantas you can really make yourself at home on an international jet-flight. (Qantas has had **46 years** experience in mixing friendliness with efficiency.) See your travel agent.

Or telephone Qantas.

AUSTRALIA'S ROUND-WORLD AIRLINE

QANTAS

46 YEARS OF DEPENDABLE SERVICE

A

B

The Ansett-ANA's "Demeanour" in Uniform section offers these rules:

Hostesses must not run in uniform, especially on the tarmac in sight of passengers. This would look undignified.

Chewing gum or sweets must not be consumed whilst on duty in view of the Public. Hostesses are not permitted to knit in view of the Public.

Smoking in uniform is not permitted with the following exceptions: one cigarette is allowed after lunch and dinner when dining in a suitable restaurant, but never in the cabin or buffet of an aircraft.

"Coffee, Tea or Me?" Popularizes Notion of Naughty Stewardess

In the popular literature of this decade stewardesses were treated as sex objects. Tomes from previous decades had featured attendants as brave heroines saving passengers from certain death in plane crashes. Stewardesses were celebrated for their professionalism and their knowledge. All that changed with a book called "Coffee, Tea or Me?" published in 1967. It described the wild lifestyles and sexual conquests of flight attendants, and constitutes a watershed in the public's attitude.

In the 1950s, the ideal stewardess was a competent, attractive wife-in-training; by the close of the 1960s stewardesses were perceived as promiscuous, young sex-kittens-of-the-sky. This new image had direct implications for the women aloft. Flight attendants were pinched and patted by male passengers who felt encouraged to act out their sexual fantasies. One airline executive reportedly said, "the girls might get patted, but they move too fast to get pinched!"

As long as images of the sexy stewardess sold seats, the airlines and the ad agencies bombarded consumers with them. With the introduction of the huge 747, more drastic campaigns and shifts in public perception were imminent.

A

B

C

A

C

B

D

E

D
TWA's **"Foreign Accent"** New York hostess pajamas
were loose and comfortable and made of paper.
Credit: "Photo: Johanna Omelia. Model: Alexandra
Hagedorn. Makeup: Lora"

E
TWA's "Foreign Accent" **French gold lamé party
dress** was also made of paper. Credit: "Photo:
Johanna Omelia. Model: Alexandra Hagedorn.
Makeup: Lora"

Introducing the Air Strip

We had a girl go through the motions to show you just what's coming off at Braniff International.

As in the picture below, our hostess appears at the airport wearing a reversible cold-weather coat, matching gloves and boots and, if it's raining, an ingenious plastic helmet.

When she boards our airplane, she
Zip
sheds these outer garments to greet you in a raspberry suit and color co-ordinated shoes.

This ensemble is too expensive to risk soiling during dinner, so at the appropriate moment, she
Zip
Snap
Zip

changes into a lovely serving dress which we call a Puccino (named for its creator, Emilio Pucci, who believes that even an airline hostess should look like a girl).

After dinner, our hostess *Zip* slips out of the Puccino, revealing the way-out outfit on the right.

Each change is made in a flash, which allows her to give you constant attention, from the time you take off to the time you land.

If the flight seems all too short, that's the whole idea.

Braniff International
Flies United States Mexico South America

In 1965, Braniff launched "**The Air Strip.**" The campaign featured Pucci-clad hostesses doing a mini striptease aloft. The industry changed radically; skirt lengths shortened and campaigns grew bold as the sexual revolution hit the skies. Credit: "Courtesy Harding Lawrence/Braniff International"

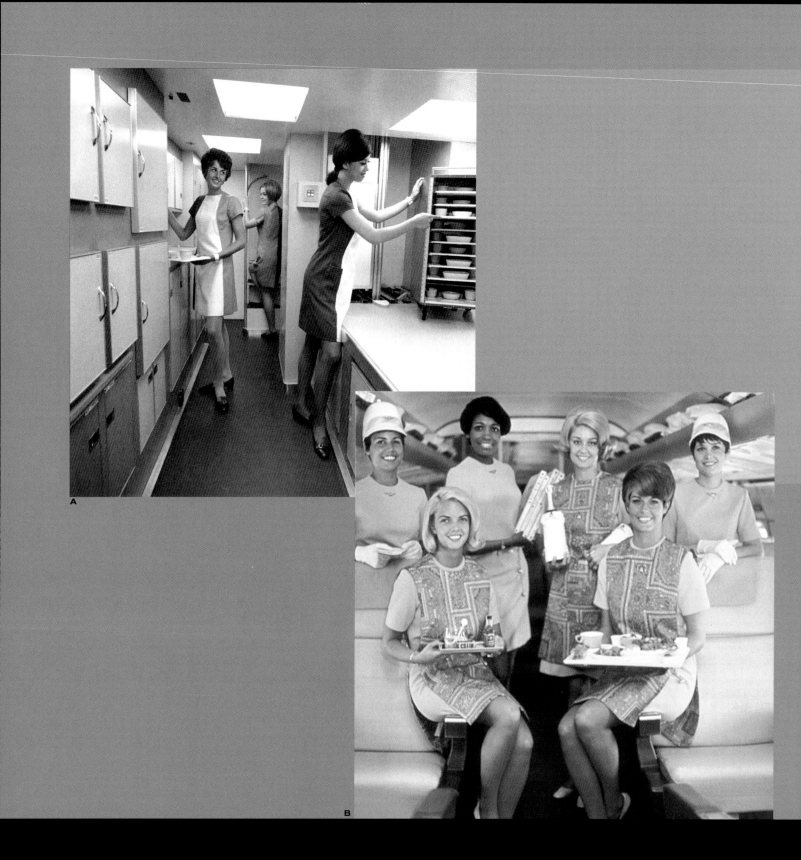

A
United's DC-10 galleys were s**pacious, modern, and
well equipped** to serve several hundred passengers.
Credit: "United Airlines Archives"

B
"No floor show. Just a **working girl working**" was the
ad tagline that helped launch these Delta uniforms.
Credit: "Courtesy of Delta Air Transport Heritage Museum"

B

A

D
Passengers could read flight attendants **like a book**
in this destination-oriented top. Credit: "Photo:
Johanna Omelia. Model: Alexandra Hagedorn.
Makeup: Lora"

E
This Ansett hostess uniform featured hot
pants worn under a **split skirt.** Credit:
"Photo Courtesy Ansett Australia"

Ch 5

The 1970s

Fly Me Girls Meet the ERA

Mealtime, 1970s-style, still featured a fabric tray cover, metal utensils and service with a smile. Credit: "Courtesy of the American Airlines C. R. Smith Museum"

Lounges, Movies, and Scantily-Clad Women Sell Seats

In 1970, the first "jumbo jet," Boeing's vast 747, was placed into service. Most models were fitted out for between 300 and 400 people with substantial space allocated for baggage, freight, and mail. Entertainment became a key enticement for getting more passengers aboard. In-flight movies were shown, and luxurious lounges with exotic themes became more prevalent than they had been in the 1950s. Upstairs, first class passengers could book tables for dinner, gather around a piano for a song or two, or sink into a cushy couch to get chummy with fellow passengers over cocktails.

More and More Luxury Aloft

In 1971, Braniff introduced its new 747 service from Dallas to Honolulu, which featured 54 first class chairs, 268 coach chairs, seven galleys, and four movie screens. "You are no longer confined to your seats," stated the 747 Braniff Place brochure. "You are invited to roam the two main aisles, stop in one of the ten conversation areas, or sit in one of the six lounges. Three of the lounges are reserved just for coach passengers and they're all handsomely furnished with comfortable chairs and couches." Braniff also offered a wahini rum welcome punch, a choice of entrees served on china plates, complimentary wine with meals, and a ten channel stereo in coach. Fourteen hostesses served on this 747.

The centerpiece of this good times atmosphere was the stewardess. In 1971, the head of one major airline opined that stewardesses should be more like Geisha girls, prepared to flatter and entertain male passengers. And so many did, particularly in print.

The "Fly Me" Campaign

National Airlines' "I'm Cheryl. Fly Me" campaign was the most notable of the early 1970s. The print ads featured close-ups of pretty young women's faces, their name and the strongly sexual invitation "fly me." The names of the women were painted on the planes like a girlfriend's name tattooed on a sailor.

The words "fly me" soon made it into the lexicon of popular culture. In the U.S. and abroad, "fly me" became the catch phrase for all sexual innuendo; it became a pick up line in one arena and a war cry for feminists in another. In 1975, the British rock band 10cc did a song called "I'm Mandy Fly Me" whose lyrics tell of adventure aloft. Fly me also launched a series of raunchy movies of the same name with themes ranging from naughty to weird. "The airline serves three wild dishes — take your choice," read one tagline. "See stewardesses battle Kung Fu Killers!" read another. "Swingin' Stewardesses" vied with movies like "Naughty Stewardesses," and "Bedroom Stewardesses" to present flight attendants as boozy, sex-crazed party girls who engaged in orgies — preferably in plane bathrooms — at the drop of a hat. A vast collection of popular culture literature used new terms like the "Mile High Club" and "Sky Sluts."

Trolling for the International Businessman

In terms of using staff as bait, National's campaign was highly effective and bookings went up 20 percent. SAS and TWA started to advertise their staff by name and destination to attract male passengers, while Iberia promised men that they would be served by their "pretty little blonde from Barcelona."

A

C

A

B

North of the border, Air Canada dressed flight attendants in this natty ensemble, which was comprised of over a dozen pieces. Credit: "Courtesy Air Canada"

C

Air Canada also offered these outfits, which reflected the popular look in 1973. Credit: "Courtesy Air Canada"

World Airways featured the "world's most beautiful stewardess" in one ad. The text said that although their attendant hadn't won a beauty contest, "we'll stick our necks out to say that she's the prettiest stewardess in our covey of 300...girls like Becky have helped us prove that service on charter flights can be just as attractive as the price."

In the East, Malaysian Airline System (MAS) discussed the "attitude of the Golden Girls" in their ad copy. "They really do care about you. Because Malaysian girls have always cared. Their desire to please and serve stems from a natural hospitality that is a Malaysian heritage." The visual is a smiling young woman looking demurely away from the camera. To promote its new flights to Australia, Hong Kong-based Cathay Pacific featured a man in a rustic setting surrounded by beautifully dressed, smiling young women. "Come with us to Sydney, Melbourne, and Perth in the care of flight hostesses from nine countries," it read.

In an ad from the same year at Singapore Airlines, a beautiful grinning woman looks directly into the camera, above the headline, "Up here, it's already the start of a new day...and you've another 2,000 miles still to fly. With this girl. And the longer you travel together the warmer her smile seems to grow. This girl of Singapore Airlines. At home five miles high, caring for you as only she knows how." Pan Am showed a disheveled woman in a maid's outfit in a darkened room with the tagline, "let someone else make the coffee." The text invited men to

JAL lined up a bevy of **beauties on the tarmac** in their brand new 1970 uniforms. Credit: "Courtesy Japan Airlines"

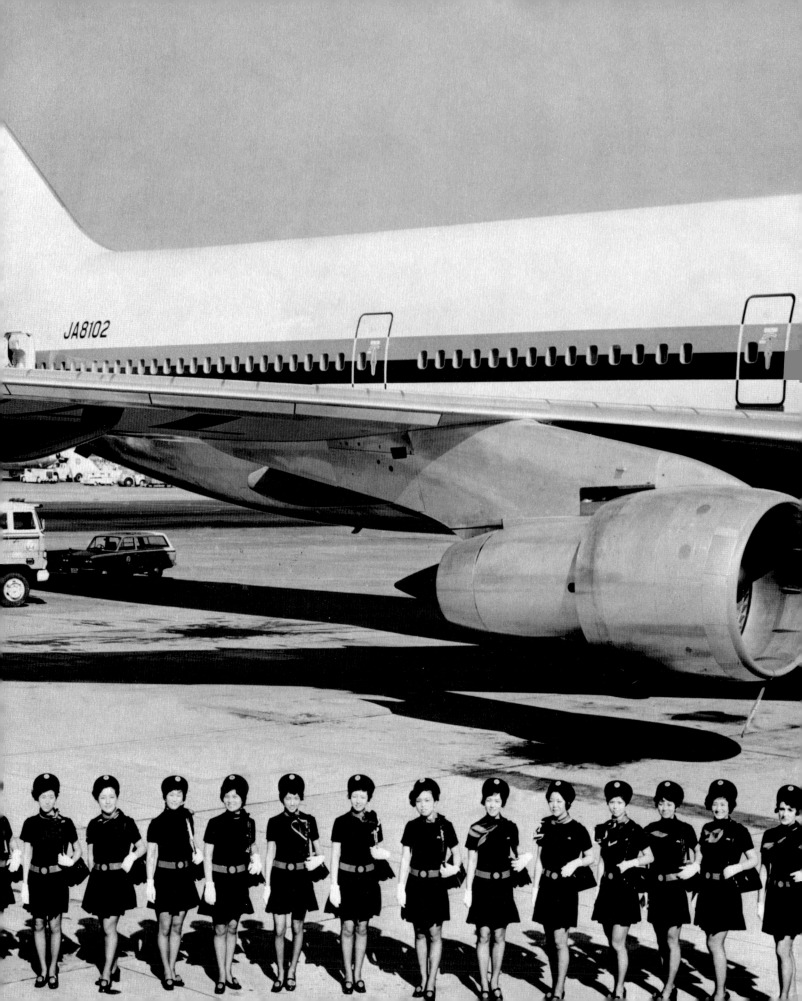

call for a free booklet called "Bachelor Party that's full of hot bargain tours." Eastern gave men "little black books" to fill with women's phone numbers on their flight to Miami.

Eastern, in 1970, showed an illustration of women's legs and bathing suit clad bottoms with the rest of their bodies obscured by beach umbrellas. "Fly to where the birds are," ran the text, birds being the British slang for women.

Other Interesting Bait

Other airlines devised elaborate in-flight themes to lure passengers aboard. Alaska Airlines, creators of the Gold Rush flights, changed over to the Golden Samovar Service in the early 1970s for their new flights to Russia in both First Class and Coach. Hostesses wearing Cossack tunics or black wool, floor length coats with foot-high hats offered exotic Russian foods like caviar and Chicken Kiev and "special beverages" served from a samovar on this service. Indeed, food in First Class became the focus of most major airlines with carriers like Portugal's TAP serving pheasant, caviar, and other delicacies on every flight.

New Planes Impact Industry

In Europe, the British and the French joined forces to develop Super Sonic Transportation (SST) technology which debuted in the 1970s. The Concorde was built, and British Airways and Air France launched 14 Concordes into the skies. They crossed the Atlantic in record time, but the jet was not judged economically viable for U.S. carriers. After a series of tests, the U.S. government concluded that the American public would never accept noisy sonic booms as a part of everyday life.

The Changing Faces of Crew and Passengers

In 1973, a pilot named Emily Howell became the first female pilot on a scheduled American airline at Frontier Airlines. American and Eastern Airlines soon followed with women pilots. They were hired thirty years after U.S., British, and Canadian women had proven their competence by flying fighters and bombers in World War II.

The faces of flight attendants were changing, too. In 1971, years after the Civil Rights Act had been passed, the U.S. Supreme Court ruled that men could not be denied jobs as flight attendants. One fifth of the flight attendants graduating in the U.S. in 1973 were men.

Male flight attendants wore military-inspired uniforms — no hot pants or sexy paper outfits for the guys! Women's uniforms had to be redesigned too, back to a more professional image. In 1974, American Airlines hired Bill Blass to create a more classic look for their attendants; 1974 saw Halston redesign Braniff uniforms in ultra-suede, and Stan Herman bring a stylish look to TWA crew. Other renowned designers including Valentino lowered skirt lengths to bring a more refined look to the uniforms.

Airways Abroad

All over the world, the faces of passengers were changing as much as the flight attendants'. British entrepreneur Sir Freddie Laker introduced "Skytrain" service from London to New York and Miami at just $75-$100 one way, making trans-Atlantic travel popular for the masses. As increased global competition forced some airlines to compete on the basis of price, the business traveler still wanted to get to his destination faster. The first Super Sonic Transports (SST) came into service as Air France

and British Airways began trans-Atlantic operations with the Concorde. Braniff, too, flew Concorde to London and Paris. The jet set moved on to become the Concorde set.

Overseas, particularly in industrializing economies, national airlines were emerging as symbols of a country's status in the world community. Flight attendants were dressed in traditional garb, reflecting their country's culture and social mores, and they served local cuisine. The magic carpet ride of foreign travel started the moment you entered the plane. The glamour of international travel was dramatically reinforced by the quality of these new players.

OPEC Crisis, Hijackers, and Deregulation

Some aspects of international travel were far from glamorous. In the 1970s, the price of oil went skyrocketing. Airlines flew their planes slower to conserve fuel because of the OPEC oil price increases. The 1970s also saw a rash of hijackers storming the airways.

B

There's something new on Alaska Airlines.

Terrorism of this kind started the previous decade, but as incidents increased, flight attendants now learned about hijackers as a part of their in-flight safety training. Ticket prices increased to pay for additional airport security. The Airline Deregulation Act of 1978 impacted the entire industry. Flight attendants saw a moratorium on hiring as carriers experienced bankruptcies, mergers and acquisitions, start-ups, and domicile closures.

Flight Attendants Still Popular with Public

Though U.S. marketing ploys and dress codes had been toned down, flight attendants were no less celebrated as a cultural phenomenon. *Cosmopolitan* magazine featured articles about becoming flight attendants, and the popular press continued its coverage of women cabin crew. On television, an episode of the phenomenally popular "Charlie's Angels" featured the fetching sleuths disguised as flight attendants to help a trainer of flight attendants identify a murderer. Little girls could play with a Barbie doll in flight attendant garb (pilot Barbie would be introduced in the 1990s!).

Legal Rights for Female Flight Attendants

By the end of the 1970s, the time was right for a less sexually overt icon of the air. The Equal Rights Amendment (ERA), a proposed amendment to the U.S. Constitution that sought to ensure equality of rights for women under the law, had been ratified by some states in the early 1970s (although, ultimately, not by the req-uisite 38 states). Feminist issues were openly discussed. The public embraced the women flight attendants' more professional look and no-nonsense attitude.

Flight attendants now reflected both sexes, and a wider span of ages. Those who had been "retired" by the airlines could now be rehired by court order. In 1971, the "no marriage rule" for women flight attendants was struck down and married women were allowed to work as the male cabin crew had always been.

In 1973, the Association of Flight Attendants (AFA) was organized to look after the rights of flight attendants. This predominantly female work force also saw a series of legal victories achieved by the AFA. In 1974, one prominent airline was forced to pay its female employees on the same scale of wages as its male employees. In 1975, AFA challenged the "no pregnancy" rule of the industry. In 1979, the AFA persuaded major airlines to "liberalize" their weight policies for female flight attendants.

In the span of one decade, female flight attendants had evolved from fly me girls to competent career women in an ever-expanding field.

A

B

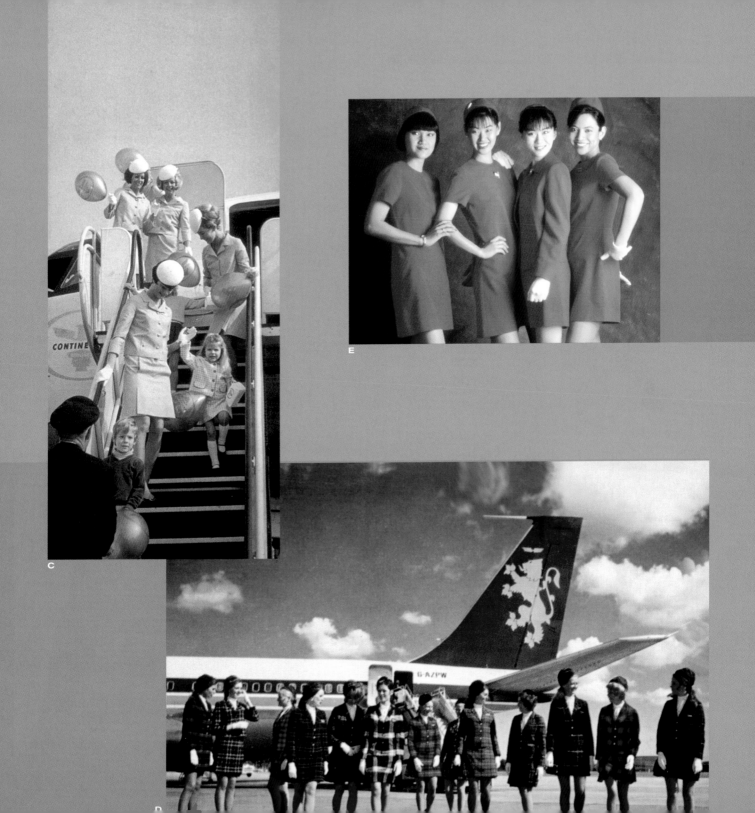

C

E

D

A

B

Now.
Japan's most beautiful gardens blossom aboard the world's most spacious jet.

Starting this summer, during EXPO '70, the first of eight JAL 747 jets will cross the Pacific. Outside it will be the biggest commercial airliner ever developed. Inside it will feature the most extraordinary decor ever created.

For each section of this spacious jet will have one of our country's most beautiful features: the Japanese Garden.

First Class will have the elegant Garden of Wisteria with an upstairs lounge called Teahouse of the Sky.

In Economy, you can choose from one of three unique sections: the Gardens of Wild Orange, Pine or Maple. Each has decor all its own and individualized service. More comfort, too. Thanks to wider seats and stand-up headroom everywhere.

There will be wide screen movies, stereo entertainment and the finest of international beverages and cuisine.

Best of all, there will be more of what legends are made of – our lovely hostesses in kimono who will pamper you throughout your flight. And introduce you to the subtle delights of Japanese comfort and hospitality.

Your travel agent is now accepting reservations for our maiden flight. Be one of the first to reserve a seat in the garden of your choice on our new 747 Garden Jet.

JAPAN AIR LINES 747 Garden Jet

D

C

E

D

F

E

C

B

D

A

C

D

A

B

D

A variety of **patterns, materials, and skirt lengths** were represented in these mid-1970s Continental ensembles. Credit: "Photos courtesy of Continental Airlines"

E

In 1975, THAI added **Western-style** lavender outfits to its collection of more traditional uniforms. Credit: "Courtesy THAI"

F

On TAP, **the menus were extensive** and the food was gourmet. Presentations like this were among the most stylish in the air. Credit: "Courtesy TAP-Air Portugal Museum"

A
United's **first woman pilot** smiled from the cockpit
in 1978 Credit: "United Airlines Archives"

B
PSA cabin staff reflected the atmosphere of the
airline that was **known for its smile.** Credit: "Photo
courtesy of US Airways Group"

C
For flight attendants everywhere, waiting for
that **late flight** was just a part of the game.
Credit: "Photo: Johanna Omelia. Model:

D

E

F

Fly the Orient Express Way

Nobody gets your Orient trip off to such a flying start

Hot oshibori towels, cocktails, Kuchitori hors d'oeuvres, wines, dinner, dessert, exotic liqueurs, movies*, stereo* . . . nobody else makes it seem like such a short trip.

Nobody else gives you the choice of mid-Pacific, north-Pacific or polar routes, flies direct from more U.S. cities, and has more 747s to the Orient.

Fly the Orient Express Way to Tokyo, Osaka, Seoul, Okinawa, Taipei, Manila, Hong Kong. Nobody else does it nearly so well.

*$2.50 charge on International 747 Flights.

NORTHWEST ORIENT 747

Ch 6

The 1980s 1990s and Beyond

Flight Attendants Stress Safety and Service

In the U.S., the 1980s saw a strong economy with a record number of passengers in the air. Consumers enjoyed greater availability of service and lower ticket prices from international, national, and regional carriers.

Mergers and acquisitions characterized the decade. The airline industry was deregulated in 1978 and two years later, competition amongst carriers had become intense. Dozens of little airlines — mostly no-frills carriers — cropped up around the U.S. and vied with established airlines to secure new and profitable routes. The new airlines served smaller cities and provided ongoing service to other destinations which had not been linked before 1980. Those unable to compete in this new world of commercial aviation filed for Chapter 11; some restructured and recovered like Continental. Other giants like Pan Am and Braniff went out of business entirely.

With less leg room, appalling snacks, and minimal in-flight service, no frills flights inspired many a joke in the early 1980s. A standard quip of the decade went, "you know you're flying a no-frills airline if the pilot asks you to chip in for gas!"

Laughs Aloft

In a marketplace where value was king, some airlines sought to define themselves by their in-flight service. A low cost carrier known for their superior service, Southwest Airlines is famous for their humorous safety announcements aloft. Some examples:

"There may be fifty ways to leave your lover, but there are only four ways out of this airplane...."

"The flight crew will be offering you beverages and a snack later in the flight....If you need anything else, we'll be up front gossiping and filing our nails."

"Who knows what you're going to find in the seat pocket in front of you at this time of day, but somewhere in there — alongside the diapers, the peanut wrappers and the empty cups — there should be a card with emergency exit information."

"Weather at our destination is 50 degrees with some broken clouds, but they'll try to have them fixed before we arrive."

The announcements serve to calm nervous passengers while making sure that frequent fliers — who have heard the safety instructions countless times — actually listen!

"Waitress in the Sky"

As the glamour of flying waned, and flight delays, crowded airports, and minimal in-flight service became the norm, some passengers became more vocal about the hassle that flying represented to them. The Replacements' 1985 album "Tim" featured a song called "Waitress in the Sky" which expressed some of the public's frustration with the airlines and their staff in the 1980s:

*"She don't wear no pants, she don't wear no tie
Always on the ball, she's always on strike
Strutting up the hall, big deal you get to fly
You ain't nothing but a waitress in the sky...."*

Some strong language about bad attitudes aloft and shoddy in-flight service comprise the rest of the lyrics of this popular tune.

A

C

B

A

B

C

Airline Landmark Goes

In New York City, the highly visible Pan Am building stood proud as one of the foremost architectural airline landmarks in the country. Helicopters to and from Kennedy Airport landed on the roof of the Pan Am building for years, a constant reminder of the importance of flight in the daily lives of Americans. With the bankruptcy of Pan Am, the building was sold, and the Pan Am name left the skyline of New York City.

Customer Loyalty Addressed

The airlines came up with one effective way to ensure customer loyalty in the 1980s — frequent flier clubs. Many of the clubs were initiated in the previous decade, but they really blossomed in the 1980s as passengers were rewarded with better benefits for the points they accrued from travel, including free flights or upgrades to First Class. Frequent flier programs could also allow you to pre-board the plane, have addition bonus points allotted to your account, or countless other promotional perks.

The Life and Stats of U.S. Flight Attendants

Flight attendants used computers to improve their jobs as computing became a function of everyday life. Computer rooms were set up in domiciles, allowing flight attendants to trade work days and bid for advance schedules.

A

B

C

In 1985, there were 63,496 flight attendants on U.S. scheduled airlines. According to an AFA membership survey, 29 percent of that total was aged between 30 to 34, and 30 percent from 35 to 39. By 1989, the median service of flight attendants had risen to seven years from two years a decade earlier. The median age of a flight attendant was 34. Most were either married or divorced, 43 percent had children and 14 percent were male. Greater earning power was achieved by the close of the decade, as were better benefits. The best-paid senior flight attendants were earning close to $40,000 a year; about half of the attendants earned between $20,000 and $30,000 yearly.

And, for U.S.-based flight attendants, the perks were still enticing. Seventy percent of flight attendants took four or more pleasure trips a year as they flew free on their own airline and at reduced air fares on other airlines. In-flight, there were more passengers to serve on long-haul flights, but the newer aircrafts like the Boeing 757 and 767 had much improved galley systems. With carts pre-loaded with food, flight attendants no longer had to run from the galley to the passengers serving trays two at a time.

Mile High Style; Bow Ties Galore

Fashion and design were still a concern for some of the airlines. Ralph Lauren designed uniforms with midi-length skirts for TWA which *Vogue* magazine heralded as a major success. Elsewhere in the U.S. and Europe, the little navy blue suit with ubiquitous bow tie typified the professional look for women in the 1980s workplace.

A

B

D

E

F

Ads Stress Professionalism

Advertisements in the Western world in the 1980s moved away from the appeal of the flight attendant and focused on her professionalism. In 1980, American Airlines featured an ad picturing a flight attendant in a blue blazer, her hands casually crossed over the headrest of a chair so that her wedding ring is apparent. She has a quote and under it, her full name with the title "Flight Attendant" following. The text refers to the corporation's long history and excellent training of flight attendants. "It takes the best people to make the best airline," the ad concludes.

European and Asian Airlines

In Europe, there was equally tough competition between the airlines. Flight attendants had less free time, more responsibilities and longer working hours. Sometimes flights were 18 hours long because of the huge distances covered by jumbo jets.

In 1984, Lufthansa lauded its on time arrivals in print ads. Air France talked about the excellence of their fleet. TWA discussed the luxurious ambiance and gourmet meals on its Royal Ambassador Service in First Class.

In Asia, Korean Air Lines asked in print, "Have you ever flown with people who treat you like an honoured guest?" showing a picture of a woman in traditional dress putting a blanket over two sleeping children. Garuda Indonesian Airways focused on the cultural aspects of their exotic destinations. THAI talked of the

Health and Safety for Flight Attendants

The AFA achieved a series of milestones in the cabin crew's health and safety in the 1980s. In 1981, the Association lobbied to maintain the number of cabin attendants per aircraft. In 1984, the FAA (after prodding by the AFA) issued a number of new safety requirements, including floor level exit lights and less flammable cabin interiors. In 1987, after a number of accidents aloft, the AFA succeeded in limiting the number of carry-on bags allowed on board; in 1988, a smoking ban was established on all domestic flights of two hours or less.

Flight Attendant Safety Professionals' Day Ushers in 1990s

In 1990, U.S. President George Bush honored flight attendants by proclaiming that July 19, 1990, was officially Flight Attendant Safety Professionals' Day. The proclamation reads, in part, "The men and women who serve as flight attendants carry out their duties with an outstanding degree of dedication. Their behavior has been calm and professional during accidents, hijackings, in-flight fires...and other situations of potential or immediate danger to human life. This tradition of professionalism has saved many passengers from injury or death and continues to increase the margin of safety for those who travel the airways today."

Cabin Pressure in the 1990s

Flight attendants certainly needed that tradition of professionalism to cope with a phenomenon called Air Rage which surfaced in the 1990s. The term refers to passen-

A **United** attendant fastens her wings with pride.

Credit: "United Airlines Archives"

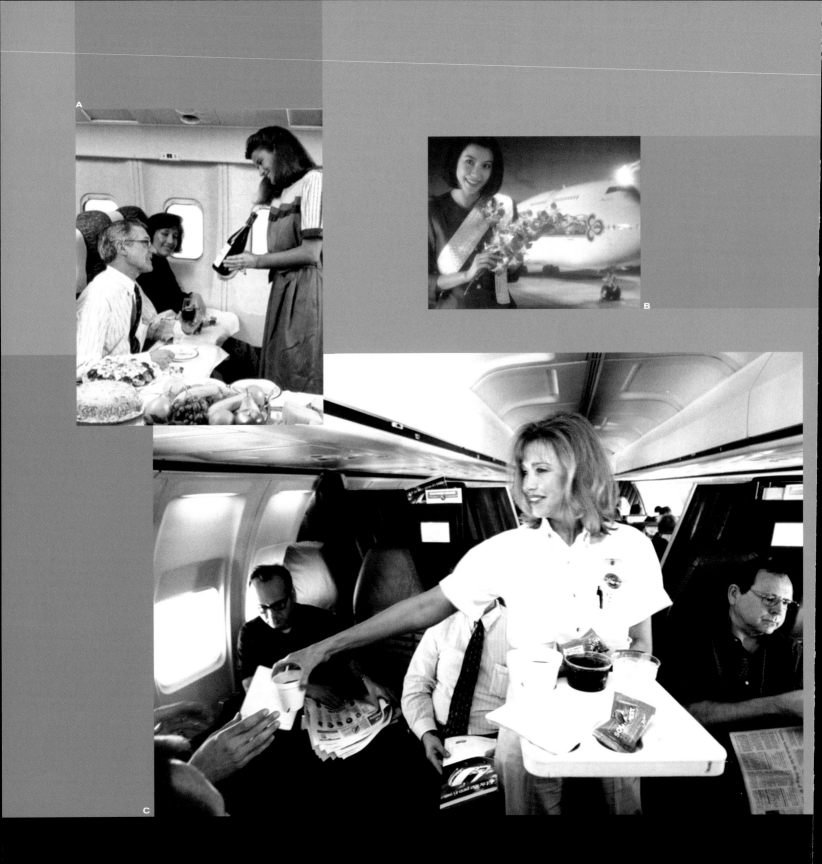

A
A selection of **gourmet delights** and fine wines
greet the TAP First Class traveler. Credit: "Courtesy
TAP-Air Portugal Museum"

B
Each THAI plane is named by the **King of Thailand**
and blessed by the Supreme Patriarch before its first
flight. Credit: "Courtesy THAI"

C
Southwest Airlines, the premier low-cost carrier, still
having fun after almost thirty years of operations.
Credit: "Courtesy Southwest Airlines"

the decade. In 1996, the FAA issued an advisory circular to flight attendants which discussed the problem in broad terms. In 1997, the first International Conference on Disruptive Airline Passengers was held, which discussed why these incidents occur and legal measures carriers can use to curtail them. Air rage, they found combines antisocial behavior, the use of alcohol, and perceived loss of control. Ground rage is another recently defined psychological phenomenon. Passengers bumped from flights due to over-booking, delays, and overcrowded airports can all contribute to this. Government agency research indicates that one quarter of air rage incidents involve alcohol; 16 percent are provoked by disputes over seat assignments; 10 percent are smokers who can't smoke. The rest of the incidents are fueled by disputes with flight attendants over carry-on luggage, and complaints about the food. With bigger planes carrying more and more passengers on the drawing board, the ramifications for flight attendants are grave.

Delivering Babies and Blessing Aircraft

Meanwhile, in Southeast Asia, the cabin crew faced different kinds of challenges. According to a brochure celebrating Thai Airways International (THAI)'s 40th anniversary, that Bangkok-based airline still has a "stringent selection process" to recruit the friendliest, most outgoing and service-minded crew. The staff has two months basic training in a classroom and full scale mock-up cabins. A six-month on-the-job training follows. Their cabin crew colleagues then supervise the attendants.

"THAI's staff are trained to stay calm and in control even during emergencies. First aid courses are part of our cabin crew training. So when a baby was born on a THAI flight from Tokyo to Bangkok a few years ago, the cabin crew assisted the mother with delivery. Dararusmee, THAI's first baby girl, was born safely and named after the aircraft."

THAI, with its modern fleet of Airbus A330s, Boeing 747s, and 777s, still has some charming age-old traditions. While the safety of each aircraft lies mainly in the hands of the pilots and cabin crew, THAI has a custom "to honor and safeguard each new aircraft." H. M. The King bestows a Royal name to each aircraft before delivery. "Upon arrival, it is blessed and anointed in a religious ceremony presided over by the Supreme Patriarch." As a parting gift, all the women on board THAI flights are given a fresh orchid corsage.

Demure Young Ladies of the Skies

On Malaysia Airlines (MAS), the ratio of four females to one male flight crew was maintained through the 1990s. "The stewardesses are more attractive," said the flight services manager in *Airborne: The Evolution and Birth of Malaysia Airlines*. "Passengers are more amenable to service by demure young ladies and experience suggests we are doing the right thing."

In 1992, the average age of MAS flight attendants, called Golden Girls, was 22. "Once they reach 23 or 24, they come to the crossroads," explained one Training Check Personnel. "Marriage is often on their minds and in the course of flying, they meet a wide variety of people, some of whom could be prospective husbands." The flight attendants on MAS still dress in traditional sarong kebaya and the airline maintains its reputation for service and reliability.

United's First Class food service.
Credit: "United Airlines Archives"

New Airlines Launch in U.S.

At the close of the 20th Century, new airlines were still cropping up. And — East or West — it is still the flight attendant who ensures passenger comfort and safety, and defines her or his carrier to the public.

JetBlue initiated operations in 1999 and launched its first flight in February 2000. This New York City-based carrier has become well known for its low fares, luxurious planes outfitted with leather seats, free 24- channel LiveTV, and its friendly, fashionable flight attendants.

"This was an airline with no history to it," said Stan Herman, JetBlue uniform designer who also designed TWA's 1974 look. "JetBlue wanted a look to suggest the quintessential New York airline. My whole concept was an all-in-one look with no jacket in the darkest, inkiest blue." The Prada-esque uniform was recognized by the Fashion Institute of Technology in an exhibition entitled "Work in Uniform: Dressed for Detail."

JetBlue flight attendants are as well-trained as they are well-dressed. All attendants receive comprehensive instruction on in-flight emergencies including CPR/automated external defibrillator training. JetBlue also offers another innovative safety feature, telemedicine services, allowing them to consult directly with board certified physicians who specialize in in-flight emergency medicine 24 hours a day, Yoga instruction is also offered aloft, a response to the dangers of deep vein thrombosis which came to light in 2001. The flying nurses of the 1930s have come full circle in the new millenium as health and medical preparedness aloft become a new focus of commercial aviation.

More Health and Safety Milestones for Flight Attendants

In the year 2000, the AFA had a number of legislative victories affecting the 106,000-plus U.S. flight attendant workforce. OSHA became involved in directing the health standards on board aircraft, ensuring that the same standards of health issues — air quality, waste disposal, disinfecting common areas — are applied aboard aircraft. The FAA had formerly been in charge of health standards aloft since the 1970s.

Terror in the Skies

In September 2001, the nightmare of aviation hijacking resurfaced in its most horrific form when terrorists commandeered four commercial U.S. aircraft and used them as flying bombs. Thousands of innocent people from all over the world died in the crashes in New York City, Washington, D.C., and Pennsylvania. The heinous crime did serve to bring the topic of security to light as an important issue for the future of commercial aviation. Newcomer JetBlue responded to the incident immediately by lining their cockpit doors with bullet-proof Kevlar and securing them so that they could only be opened on the cockpit side. In November 2001, the Aviation Security Bill was passed, a bill tightening up security both on the ground and in the air. Some of the major issues addressed by this legislation included federalizing the security screening workforce, expanding the federal sky marshal program, and reinforcing all cockpit doors. In 2002, the AFA continued to address aircraft cabin security by working with the airlines to establish significant self-defense training programs as a requisite for flight attendants.

Malaysia Airline System (MAS) attendants in their
1986 updated sarong kebaya. Credit: "Courtesy of

A

B

A

B

An **Airbus A380** equipped with work stations for the 24-hour efficiency demanded of today's executives. Credit: "Courtesy Airbus"

C

Chairs fold out into **beds** in this Airbus A380 mock up. Credit: "Courtesy Airbus"

D

Dining bars are **sleek, elegant,** and **well-lighted.** Credit: "Courtesy Airbus"

The **Airbus A380,** the new plane for the next generation
of flight attendants. Credit: "Courtesy Airbus"